The Battle for Rama

The Battle for Rama

Case of the Temple at Ayodhya

Meenakshi Jain

Aryan Books International
New Delhi

THE BATTLE FOR RAMA
Case of the Temple at Ayodhya

ISBN: 978-81-7305-579-9

First published: 2017

Reprinted in **2024** by
Aryan Books International
Pooja Apartments, 4B, Ansari Road, New Delhi-110 002 (India)
Tel.: 23287589, 23255799; Fax: 91-11-23270385
E-mail: aryanbooks@gmail.com
www.aryanbooks.com

Designed and Printed in India by
ABI Prints & Publishing Co., New Delhi

Contents

List of Illustrations vii

1. Introduction 1
2. Babur in Ayodhya 11
3. Accounts of Foreign Travellers and British Administrators 17
4. Attempts to Reclaim Sacred Spaces 34
5. Muslim Sources on Ramjanmabhumi/Babri Masjid 48
6. The Conflict at Ayodhya Documented 53
7. Left Historians Intervene 78
8. Hindu Sources on Rama Worship and the Janmabhumi Temple 88
9. Pillar Bases – the First Archaeological Evidence 94
10. A Gahadavala Inscription Recovered and Treta Ka Thakur Re-discovered 103
11. Left Historians and the ASI Report 116

12. No Mention of Babri Masjid in the Revenue Records 136
13. The Allahabad High Court Judgement on the Ramjanmabhumi/Babri Masjid Case 140

Select Bibliography 147
Index 157

List of Illustrations

1. A view of Ayodhya, painting by William Hodges, 1785.
2. The Alamgiri Mosque at Ayodhya which stands on land in possession of Hanuman Garhi since 1765.
3. Babri Masjid, Ayodhya.
4. Babur's mosque at Panipat.
5. Mir Hindu Beg's mosque at Sambhal.
6. Wash drawing of Sambhal mosque by Thomas Daniell and William Daniell, 1789.
7. Title page of Samuel Purchas's book, *Purchas His Pilgrimage*.
8. Title page of de Laet's book.
9. Title page of Thomas Herbert's book.
10. Joseph Tieffenthaler's map of the Ganges and Ghaghara rivers.
11. Sketch by Joseph Tieffenthaler.
12. Sketch by Joseph Tieffenthaler.
13. Sketch by Joseph Tieffenthaler.
14. Sketch by Joseph Tieffenthaler.
15. Sketch by Joseph Tieffenthaler.

16. Patrick Carnegy's map of Ayodhya, 1870.
17. A drawing of the Kashi Vishvanath temple after its demolition, by James Prinsep in 1826.
18. A photograph of the back side of the Gyanwapi mosque which rests on part of the Kashi Vishvanath temple.
19. The Madanmohan temple, Vrindavan as published in F.S. Growse's *Mathura: A District Memoir*, 1882.
20. The Gobind Dev temple converted into a mosque. The *mehrab* is visible on top (photo by John Murray, c. 1850).
21. Report of the *thanedar* of Awadh dated 28th November 1858 on *havan* and *puja* inside Babri Masjid.
22. Muhammad Asghar's complaint of 30th November 1858 on *havan* and *puja* inside Babri Masjid.
23. Report of the *thanedar* on eviction of Sikhs from Babri Masjid.
24. A 2nd-1st century BCE terracotta from Kaushambi showing Ravana carrying away Sita.
25. A terracotta figure from Nachara Khera, with the name Rama inscribed in Brahmi characters of the 3rd century CE.
26. Terracotta from Bhitargaon showing a scene from the *Ramayana*, 5th century CE, presently in Brooklyn Museum, U.S.A.
27. Ahalya offering fruits to Rama, 5th century CE, Deogarh, presently in National Museum, Delhi.
28. Ramayana scenes from the Durga temple, Aihole, Karnataka.
29. Rama, Vali, and Sugriva from the Papanatha temple, Karnataka.
30. *Vanaras*, Hoysalesvara temple, Halebid.
31. Sri Rama giving *abhignam* (ring) to Hanuman, Halebid.
32. A depiction of Rama from the Pattabhirama temple, Hampi.
33. The Hazare Rama temple, Hampi.

34. Rama and Lakshman as depicted at the Gandha Madhana hill, Hampi.
35. Akbar's Rama Siya coins.
36. Rama and Lakshmana bemoaning the loss of Sita, Pahari School, Kangra, 1780-1785.
37. The Rajim stone inscription dated AD 1145 recording the construction of a "beautiful temple" for Rama.
38. The Treta ka Thakur inscription.
39. The Vishnu Hari inscription recovered in the aftermath of 6th December 1992.

Some finds from the ASI excavations at Babri Masjid
40. Glazed ware sherds.
41. Glazed ware large bowl.
42. Porcelain ware sherds.
43. Terracotta glazed ware sherds.
44. Sprouted pot.
45. Pots from Kushan period.
46. Leg portion resting on pedestal.
47. A human leg, terracotta.
48. Torso of human figure wearing uttariya, terracotta.
49. Male holding a perforated disc, terracotta.
50. A decorated human head, terracotta.
51. Human head with large earrings, terracotta.
52. Animal head.
53. General view of the excavated trenches in the southern area.
54. North-south oriented brick wall with plastered inner face.
55. Wall of the temple with decorated architectural members.
56. Pillar bases attached to the contemporary floor 2 in northern area.
57. Circular shrine.
58. Tank like structure below Rama Chabutra.

59. Close up of *Makara-pranala* used in wall of the mosque.
60. Some of the decorated 14 stone black pillars used in Babri Masjid.
61. *Ghata*-shaped pit cut into large brick paving.

1

Introduction

The holiness of Ayodhya and its identity as Rama's birthplace was freely acknowledged in several Persian works in the medieval era. Abul Fazl Allami (1551-1602), official historian of Emperor Akbar, noted that Ayodhya was regarded as "sacred ground" and "on the ninth of the light half of the month of Chaitra a great religious festival is held." Rama was born "in the city of Ayodhya ... esteemed one of the holiest places of antiquity" (*Ain-i Akbari* III: 334, 316-17).

Another interesting reference to the *janambhumi* of Rama came from a *sanad* issued by the Mughal authorities in July 1723. Akbar had granted six *bighas* of land to Hanuman Tila at Ayodhya, on the 13th Ramzan of 1008 AH (28th March 1600).[1] The *sanad* was renewed to Sadhu Abhayarama Das on 8th July 1723, by the Superintendent of Endowments. The writer of the *sanad* stated, in Persian, that he was writing it from the "*maulud*" (*janambhumi*) of Rama. The English translation of the *sanad* stated,

> This insignificant writer, who is native of the holy place which is the *maulud* of Rama, is reducing it (the *sanad*) in

> writing with pen. By order, it is certified that six *bighas* of land in the province of Oudh which was granted for the construction of Hanuman Tila, is given to Abhayarama in the fifth exalted reign after comparing it with the deed issued on the 13th *Ramjan* of 1008 AH, i.e. 28th March, 1600 (Kunal 2016: 405-12).

The first definite reference to the *Janamsthan* (birthplace of Rama) also came from a Muslim source. On 30th November 1858, the Mutawalli of Babri Masjid, in his first petition to the British government referred to the disputed structure as *Masjid Janamsthan*; and in a subsequent appeal on 21st January 1870 as *Masjid Baburi Waqia Janmasthan*. The English translation of his first appeal said,

> *Gharib Parwar Aadil-e-Zaman Salamat* Sir,
>
> In a recent incident one Nihang Sikh resident of Punjab Sikkhan, a government employee (sic) is creating riot on Janam Sthan Masjid situated in Oudh (Allahabad High Court Judgement: pages 2300-13 para 2317).[2]

Several works in Arabic, Persian, and Urdu composed in the nineteenth century also explicitly referred to the demolition of the temple and its replacement by Babri Masjid (Narain 1993: 16-37). One such work was the *Jannah al-Mashriq wa Matla 'an-Nur al-Mashriq*, re-titled *Al-Hind-u fi al- 'Ahd al-Islami*, by Maulana Hakim Sayyid Abd al-Hayy. It was translated into Urdu by Maulana Shams Tabriz Khan, under the title *Hindustan Islami Ahd mein*. In an introduction, the author's son, Maulana Abu l-Hasan 'Ali Nadawi alias Ali Mian stated,

> And among them is the great mosque that was built by the Timurid king Babar in the sacred city of Ajodhya. It is believed that Rama Chandra considered to be the manifestation of God, was born here. There is a long story about his wife Sita. There was a big temple for them in this city. At a certain place Sita used to sit and cook food for her consort. Well, the said king Babar demolished it and built a

1. A view of Ayodhya, painting by William Hodges, 1785.

2. The Alamgiri Mosque at Ayodhya which stands on land in possession of Hanuman Garhi since 1765.

3. Babri Masjid, Ayodhya.

mosque at that very place with chiseled stone in 923 AH (Narain 1993: 16-17).

Besides medieval works in Persian and Urdu, there was the notable account of the Austrian Jesuit, Joseph Tieffenthaler (1710-1785), who travelled through Awadh between 1766 and 1771. He wrote,

> ...here was a house where Beschan (Vishnu) was born in the form of Ram. ... Subsequently Aurengzebe or Babor, according to others, got this place razed in order to deny the noble people, the opportunity of practicing their superstitions ... (pages 3503-09 para 3514).

After the British takeover of Awadh, all official records and district gazetteers of the colonial State were also unanimous that Babri Masjid occupied the site of the temple. Every British report on Ayodhya noted the black stone pillars in the mosque, all traces of images on their bases having been cut off "to satisfy the conscience of the bigot" (Martin II 1976: 333-36).

Anton Fuhrer (1853-1930), a German Indologist who served as Curator of the Lucknow Provincial Museum and was also Archaeological Surveyor of the North Western Provinces, recorded,

> The old temple of Ramachandra at Janmasthanam must have been a very fine one, for many of its columns have been used by the Musalmans in the construction of Babar's masjid. These are of strong, close-grained, dark-coloured or black stone, called by the natives *kasauti*, 'touch-stone slate,' and carved with different devices. They are from seven to eight feet long, square at the base, centre and capital, and round or octagonal intermediately (Fuhrer 1889: 68).

The *Annual Report of the Office of the Archaeological Surveyor, Northern Circle, Agra*, submitted by Maulvi Shuaib in 1906, recorded three inscriptions at Babri Masjid. Appendix D of the Report listed the inscriptions copied at that time in serial numbers 10 to 12. Inscription No. 10 was the stone slab on the outside of the central arch of the Masjid. It was in Persian, named the ruler as Babur, and the date of construction as AH 935, i.e. AD 1528. In the last column under Remarks it stated that the inscription,

> Records the erection of the mosque which was built on the same spot where the old temple of Janam Asthanam of Ram Chandra was (Kunal 2016: 171-73).

This entry raises several intriguing questions – when was the inscription put up and when was it removed? Is there any record of anyone else having seen it? Equally important, why was Maulvi Shuaib's *Annual Report of the Office of the Archaeological Surveyor, Northern Circle, Agra,* not made public for over a century?

That apart, more recently Hans Bakker, whose authoritative work on Ayodhya was published in 1986 well before the controversy erupted, wrote,

> The oldest pieces of archaeological evidence are the black columns which remain from the old (Visnu) temple that was situated on the holy spot where Rama descended to earth (Janma-bhumi). This temple was destroyed by the first Mogul prince Babur in AD 1528 and replaced by a mosque which still exists. The following specimens of these pillars are known to exist: fourteen pillars were utilized by the builder Mir Baqi in the construction of the mosque and are still partly visible within it; two pillars were placed besides the grave of the Muslim saint Fazl Abbas alias Musa Ashikhan, who, according to oral tradition, incited Babur to demolish the Hindu temple. The grave and these two pillars (driven upside-down into the ground) are still shown in Ayodhya, a little south of the Kubertila... (Bakker 1986: 44).

He added,

> ...the original birthplace temple dated from the 10th or 11th century. Before its destruction the temple must have

> been one of the main pilgrimage centres of Ayodhya, especially on the occasion of Ramanavami....The destruction of the temple would not have implied the end of all forms of worship in and around the holy site. Just as they do today, pilgrims may have assembled near the mosque to have darshan of the tirtha, and in order to perform the puja special provisions may have been made...
>
> ....The ritual of Ramanavami described in OA 22 (a recension of the *Ayodhya Mahatmya*), which is said to be carried out in the Janmasthan (OA 22.22), does not require a temple or the like and could therefore have been performed somewhere near the original holy spot in the 16th and following centuries.
>
> Such perseverance and flexibility of Hinduism under Muslim repression, which was demonstrated throughout the history of North India, could have provided an objective reason for the compiler of the OA recension not to delete or minimize his description of the Janamsthan despite its occupation by a mosque... (Bakker Part II 1986: 146-47).

In an astonishing act of daring, a handful of Left historians attempted to counter a centuries old belief, and vociferously assert that Babri Masjid was built on vacant land. They remain undeterred despite the mounting evidence stacked against them. Some of these historians even appeared as experts of the Babri Masjid Action Committee (BMAC) during negotiations between the Vishwa Hindu Parishad (VHP), BMAC, and the Government in 1990-1991. Yet throughout they have maintained the charade of being "independent historians."

In his recently published autobiography [*Njan Enna Bharatiyan* (I an Indian)], Dr. K.K. Muhammad, former Regional Director (North) of the Archaeological Survey of India (ASI), has stated that a set of Left historians systematically derailed attempts at a peaceful resolution of the issue.[3] He writes,

> A team of Left historians in Jawaharlal Nehru University such as Romila Thapar, Bipin Chandra, and S. Gopal argued that there was no mention of the dismantling of the temple before the nineteenth century and Ayodhya was a Buddhist-Jain centre. Historians such as Irfan Habib, R.S. Sharma, Athar Ali, D.N. Jha, Suraj Bhan, too joined and it became a big grouping.

The "Leftist drama," he states,

> ....instilled courage and gave false hopes to the BMAC. This resulted in a reversal of the thought process amongst Muslims who had till then, been pondering wholeheartedly about giving back the mosque and settling the matter amicably. They came to a renewed conclusion that the mosque will not be given...

The BMAC, "... held several meetings under the leadership of Irfan Habib, the then Chairman of Indian Council of Historical Research (ICHR)." Though Member Secretary, M.G.S. Narayanan opposed this, "it had little value in the presence of Habib." "The Babri issue," K.K. Muhammad states, "would have been settled long ago if the Muslim intelligentsia had not fallen prey to the brain washing of these historians" (*Deccan Chronicle* 15 January 2016; *Haindava Keralam* 16 January 2016).

The latest insider account on the tactics of Left historians comes from Kishore Kunal, Officer on Special Duty (Ayodhya) under Prime Ministers V.P. Singh and Chandra Shekhar. Kunal, incidentally a former student of both Professors R.S. Sharma and D.N. Jha has cited official correspondence to substantiate his statements (see pages 95-99 in this volume). Dismissing Left claims to impartiality, he also points out that the authors of *Ramjanmabhumi-Babri Masjid: A Historians' Report to the Nation* (13 May 1991), Professors R.S. Sharma, Athar Ali, D.N. Jha, and Suraj Bhan, all BMAC experts, while dismissive of evidence tendered by the VHP in support of its claim on the temple, made no evaluation of the documents submitted by the BMAC.[4]

Kunal notes that *Ramjanmabhumi-Babri Masjid: A Historians'Report to the Nation* falsely claimed that "... Babri Masjid became a protected monument under the Ancient Monuments Act, 1940 (re-legislated, 1958)" (Noorani I 2003: 46). Babri Masjid was, however, never declared a protected monument under the Ancient Monuments Act by the ASI. In a communication dated 2nd May 1991, the Director General (DG) of ASI, M.C. Joshi unambiguously stated,

> As the Babri Masjid is not a centrally protected monment, the Archaeological Survey of India has not so far made any detailed study of the monument (Kunal 2016: xxxv-xxxvi).

This was confirmed by Madhav Godbole, former Home Secretary, in his book *Unfinished Innings*,

> The possibility of declaring the RJB-BM structure a protected monument was considered but had to be given up as the Department of Culture and the Director General of Archaeology advised that the monument did not satisfy the criteria for declaring it as such (Godbole 1996: 375).

But what is truly astounding is Kishore Kunal's exposure on the Treta Ka Thakur inscription housed in Lucknow Museum. For over two decades, Left historians, principally Professor Irfan Habib, mounted a forceful campaign claiming that this inscription was stolen from Lucknow Museum and planted at Ayodhya during the chaos of 6th December 1992. Now for the first time a photograph of the Treta Ka Thakur inscription has been published (Kunal 2016: 306). It conclusively establishes that the Treta Ka Thakur inscription and the Vishnu-Hari inscription found in 1992 are two distinct epigraphs and that there had been no substitution (see pages 103-12 in this volume).

But does evidence really matter? Evidence may come; evidence may go; but Left historians "go on forever."

END NOTES

1. The earliest surviving revenue grant to a Hindu deity by Akbar was in January 1565, to the Gobind Rai (Govind Dev) temple at Mathura. Subsequently, a *farman* of 1598 recorded land grants to 35 named temples in Mathura and its environs (Mukherjee and Habib 1988: 235-39).

   In AD 1571 Akbar made a first grant to the Jogis of Jakhbar (of the Kanphata sect of Nath Jogis), in Gurdaspur district of Punjab. The grant was confirmed in November 1581, when Jogi Udant Nath met the Emperor personally. In 1578, another Shaiva, Chandar Nath was patronized by Akbar for the first time (Goswamy and Grewal 1967: 6-7, 21, 25-26). The Parsi, Dastur Mahrji Rana was also conferred a land grant by Akbar. Akbar's cordial relations with the great Jain Acharya, Hirvijaya Suri are also recorded. The Acharya was summoned to Akbar's court to explain the tenets of his faith. He so impressed the Emperor that he was conferred the title of *Jagat Guru* (World Teacher). In response to a request by the Acharya, the Emperor issued a *farman*, dated 6th June 1584, banning animal slaughter during twelve holy days of *Paryushana*. Another *farman* was issued in AD 1592; and was addressed to the Governors, jagirdars, and officials of Malwa, Ahmadabad, and the rest of the Empire. It stated that at the request of the Acharya, the "heaven-reaching" hills of Siddhachal, Girnar, Taranga, Keshrinath, and Abu, all situated in Gujarat, and the five hills of Rajgir, and the hill of Samat Shikhar in Bengal, together with all the *kothis* and temples below these hills, as also all other places of pilgrimage of the Jain Svetambar community throughout the Empire, should be handed over to the Jains so that no one may kill any animal on those hills or near those temples. The *farman* stated that the Emperor found this request "just and reasonable and not contrary to the (Islamic) law, ordered that the hills and temples be bestowed to Hirvijaya Suri as the Acharya was regarded the representative of the Jain Svetambar community (Commissariat 1940: 8-10). Akbar himself took vows of limited abstinence from meat-eating, saying, "Were it not for the thought of the difficulty of sustenance, I would prohibit men from eating meat. The reason why I do not altogether abandon it myself is that many others might willingly forego it likewise and be thus cast into despondency." Jahangir recorded that Akbar ate meat for three months a year, and "for the remaining nine, contented himself with Sufi food" (Findly 1987: 252-53).

In 1589, Padmasagara wrote the first known account in Sanskrit of the rise of the Mughals to power. He embedded this narrative within a poem titled *Jagadgurukavya* (Poem on the Teacher of the World), which eulogized the life of Hiravijaya Suri and his extensive ties with the Mughal court (Truschke 2012: 374). Padmasagara celebrated the effective enforcement of Akbar's orders. For example, after noting that Akbar had agreed to Hiravijaya's request to prohibit fishing in a particular lake near Fatehpur Sikri, he observed that "[glorious Padshah Akbar] ordered servants to sound drums throughout the city in order to inform all the people and secretly appointed men to arrest those who violated the rule" (Truschke 2012: 381-82).

Abul Fazl is reported to have questioned Hirvijaya Suri on the legitimacy of Islam. Jain accounts presented this exposition as Hirvijaya Suri's ability to "answer the threat of Mughal-supported Islam" (Truschke 2015: 1314-15). Akbar's *farmans* prohibiting animal slaughter do not, however, seem to have been obeyed by local officials. This was apparent from the repeated reiteration of the same order in numerous *farmans* (Krishnamurti 1961: 82-83).

2. This refers to the Allahabad High Court Judgement of 30th September 2010, delivered by Justices Sudhir Agrawal, D.V. Sharma, and S.U. Khan. Unless otherwise stated all such citations are from the ruling of Justice Agrawal.
3. For a review of K.K. Muhammad's book see *Swarajya* 7th September 2016, "Anyone who didn't agree with Irfan Habib was branded 'Hindutvawadi': Archaeologist in Autobiography".
4. A recent incident concerning the Alamgiri Masjid at Ayodhya, built in the 17th century by Emperor Aurangzeb, perhaps indicates that the Ramjanmabhumi issue could also have been settled cordially, but for the intervention of vested interests.

The structure and the land on which Alamgiri Masjid was situated came in possession of Hanuman Garhi around 1765. Nawab Shujauddaulah donated the land to Hanuman Garhi, on condition that namaaz would continue at the Masjid. Historian Roshan Taqui described the incident,

"After the battle of Buxar in 1764, Shujauddaulah, the Nawab of Awadh, moved his capital from Faizabad to Lucknow. During his reign in Faizabad he had donated the land in Ayodhya for the construction of Hanuman Garhi temple. After he shifted to Lucknow, when a delegation of Mahants visited him and appealed for more land, the Nawab donated 4 pucca bighas of land that already had on it a Masjid built by Mughal emperor Aurangzeb."

The practice of offering namaaz, however, gradually ended and the Masjid lay abandoned. The Ayodhya municipal board recently declared the dilapidated Alamgiri Masjid 'hazardous', and pasted a notice banning entry into the building. This spurred some local Muslims to meet Hanuman Garhi's chief priest, Mahant Gyan Das, and request him for permission to get the Masjid repaired.

The Hanuman Garhi temple trust not only allowed reconstruction of the Masjid, but also agreed to bear the costs and welcomed Muslims to offer namaaz in the premises (*The Times of India* 1-9-2016).

2

Babur in Ayodhya

In popular memory, the demolition of the Ramjanmabhumi temple at Ayodhya has long been associated with the Mughal Emperor Babur, as the destruction of the Krishnajanmabhumi temple at Mathura and the Vishvanath temple at Kashi have been linked to Emperor Aurangzeb. Apologists of Babur have derived relief from the fact that the pages of his *Memoirs* pertaining to that period are missing.

In 1819, the Scottish Orientalist, John Leyden (1775-1811), in his translation of the *Memoirs of Zehir-ed-din Muhammed Babur*, stated that Babur had encamped near Ayodhya on 28th March, AH 934. The translation was published in collaboration with William Erskine (1773-1852), Scottish scholar and administrator, and first secretary of the Literary Society of Bombay. As per this work, Babur recorded,

> We were still a march or two from Oudh... On Saturday, the 7th of Rajeb, I encamped two or three kos above Oudh...

An entry of 2 April, AH 934 confirmed Babur's stay in Ayodhya for a fortnight,

> I halted some days in this station, for the purpose of settling the affairs of Oudh and the neighbouring country, and for making the necessary arrangements. Seven or eight kos above Oudh, on the banks of the river Saru, is the well-known tract called the hunting ground. I sent Mir Muhammed Jalehban to examine the fords of the rivers Gogra and Saru, which he did. On Thursday, the 12th, I mounted, to set off on a hunting party (Leyden and Erskine II 1826: 332-33).

In 1922, British Orientalist, Annette S. Beveridge (1842-1929), in her translation of Babur's *Memoirs*, affirmed that Babur had encamped 72 miles north of Ayodhya on 28th March 1528,

> We stayed a few days on that ground (near Aud) in order to settle the affairs of Aud. People praised the land lying along the Sird (a; Sarayu) 7 or 8 *kurohs* (14-16 miles) above Aud, saying it was hunting ground (Beveridge II 1922: 602).

Babur's narrative broke off on 2nd April to resume on 18th September, during which period Babri Masjid was apparently constructed. Annette Beveridge presented a translation of a fragment that appeared to be a segment of the lost record of AH 934. It could have been a Persian translation of an authentic Turki piece and suggested that Babur may have stayed a little longer at Ayodhya or returned later the same year. It stated,

> After spending several days pleasantly in that place, where there are gardens, running-waters, well-designed buildings, trees, particularly mango trees, and various birds of coloured plumage, I ordered the march to be towards Ghazipur (Beveridge II 1922: 680).

Professor B.R. Grover noted that Babur again visited the eastern districts, Jaunpur territory, in May-June 1529, for which period there was no break in his *Memoirs* (Grover 2015: 244, 246).

4. Babur's mosque at Panipat.

5. Mir Hindu Beg's mosque at Sambhal.

6. Wash drawing of Sambhal mosque by Thomas Daniell and William Daniell, 1789.

While evaluating the loss of the missing pages, it bears recalling that Babur did not document every event in his life. He maintained silence, for instance, about taking help from the Safavid King, Shah Ismail, in his third attempt to capture Samarqand. According to the terms the Safavid monarch imposed, Babur, a Sunni, had to accept the trappings of the Shia creed. The creed was anathema for orthodox Sunni Muslims of Samarqand. There was not a word on this in the *Babur-Nama* (Asher 1992: 19).

MOSQUES ASSOCIATED WITH BABUR

Three mosques associated with Babur have survived in India (one of which was pulled down in 1992). Of these, one was imperially patronized, the other two constructed on Babur's orders by his nobles. All were built in the closing years of his reign. The sponsorship of these mosques was significant. For, prior to his conquest of India there was little evidence of Babur's sanctioning religious structures (Asher 1992: 25).

Babur's own mosque in Panipat was built on the site of his victory over Sultan Ibrahim Lodi which made him master of Hindustan. According to inscriptions, the mosque was well under way, if not finished, by the end of 1527; the gate, well, and garden were completed by 1528.

The mosque at Sambhal was constructed in 1526 by Babur's General, Mir Hindu Beg. It was the largest built in the Delhi region since Timur's sack of the city in 1398. Located atop a hill, it dominates the landscape for a considerable distance. The choice of Sambhal was noteworthy. According to Hindu tradition that was known to the Mughals, the last incarnation of Vishnu would appear in Sambhal at the end of the era (Asher 1992: 28). Abul Fazl Allami recorded Mughal knowledge of this Hindu belief,

> In the city of Sambal is a temple called Hari Mandal (the temple of Vishnu) belonging to a Brahman, from among

whose descendants the tenth avatar will appear in this spot (*Ain-i Akbari* II: 285).

While recording this tradition of the Kalki *avatar*, Abul Fazl was careful not to divulge that the Hari temple had been destroyed and a mosque constructed at the site with its debris. Equally, while writing about the sanctity of Pattan Somnath for Hindus, he refrained from any reference to its destruction by Mahmud Ghaznavi.

The use of temple material in the Sambhal mosque is evident in the internal architecture of the building (e.g. two rosettes on stone slabs leading from the eastern gateway to the quadrangle; the chain for hanging the temple bell, and a passage at the back for the performance of *parikarma* by worshippers, are still visible).

Babur remained quiet on this incident as well, though there was no break in his *Memoirs* for this period.[1] In September-October 1527, he visited Sambhal and stayed there for three days. The inscription on the Sambhal mosque also clearly stated that it was built by Mir Hindu Beg on the 'Farman of Shahanshah of the World' Muhammad Babur in the year December 1526 (Grover 2015: 33-34, 45, 273).[2]

The last mosque of Babur's time was built at Ayodhya. Like Sambhal, Ayodhya was a site of immense significance for Hindus as the sacred birthplace of Lord Rama. The incorporation of Hindu architectural members prominently displayed in the mosque was perhaps intended by Mir Baqi as a statement of Muslim authority (Asher 1992: 29-30).

The construction of mosques on sites associated with non-Islamic traditions was a new beginning for Babur. Before his conquest of India, he had claimed his right to sovereignty on grounds of his Timurid heritage and Turkishness, not religion. But once he had established himself in India, the establishment of Islam became an objective of his rule. He referred to Hindus as *kafirs*, and termed the war against Rana Sanga, as *jihad*, holy war. Soon after defeating Rana Sanga, he assumed the title of *Ghazi*, a soldier committed to the cause of Islam, and wrote a verse declaring his intent to overpower Hindus and pagans.[3] He thereby conformed to the long-established practices of Muslim rulers conquering non-Muslim lands. The location of the mosques at Sambhal and Ayodhya, in generally charged locales, was in conformity with the spirit of Babur's new legitimizing idiom[4] (Asher 1992: 30).

END NOTES

1. Professor R. Nath has pointed out that Babur, in his *Memoirs*, mentioned only one mosque he had constructed, that at Dholpur, which is not extant. He did not record the construction of any mosque at Delhi, Agra, Sikri, or Gwalior. Nor did he refer to the mosques at Sambhal, Panipat, Rohtak, Palam, Pilkhuwa, Maham and Sonipat, the inscriptions of which bear his name (Nath 1991: 19).
2. Hindus long associated with the Mughal court, too, retained empathy with their ancient traditions. In the 1740s, courtier and noted litterateur, Anand Ram Mukhlis accompanying the Mughal Emperor, Muhammad Shah, on a journey-cum-military expedition to the Gangetic valley, recorded his sentiments on reaching the town of Sambhal. Commenting on the transformation of the Hari Mandir into the Jami Masjid of the town, Anand Ram reasoned, "Earlier too it was a place of worship (*ibadat kanah*), and even now it is a place of worship." He noted the existence of a tank, now in poor condition, but still deemed holy by people who gathered there to bathe. Brahmins too came to recite *shlokas*. Anand Ram was moved to compose a somewhat ambivalent, but regretful verse in Persian,
   "After this, in place of tears,
   The heart comes out,
   When the pond's water dries'
   Earth comes out" (Subrahmanyam 2004: 94-96).
3. Babur gave up drinking on the eve of the battle with Rana Sangha; "What wine we had with us was poured on the ground..." (Beveridge II 1922: 551-52).

After his victory, Babur assumed the title of Ghazi,

For Islam's sake, I wandered in the wilds,
Prepared for war with pagans and Hindus,
Resolved myself to meet the martyr's death.
Thanks be to God! A ghazi I became (Beveridge II 1922: 575).

4. Babur was not enamoured of India. A much-cited entry in his *Memoirs* stated,

   Hindustan is a country of few charms. Its people have no good looks; of social intercourse, paying and receiving visits there is none; of genius and capacity none; of manners none; in handicraft and work there is no form or symmetry, method or quality; there are no good horses, no good dogs, no grapes, musk-melons or first-rate fruits, no ice or cold water, no good bread or cooked food in the bazaars, no hot-baths, no colleges, no candles, torches or candlesticks....

   Pleasant things of Hindustan are that it is a large country and has masses of gold and silver...Another good thing in Hindustan is that it has unnumbered and endless workmen of every kind... (Beveridge II 1922: 518-20).

3

Accounts of Foreign Travellers and British Administrators

Several foreign travellers and British administrators witnessed the Hindu commitment to Ayodhya and their belief that Babri Masjid was built at the site of the Ramjanmabhumi temple.

William Finch (d. 1613), agent to an expedition sent by the East India Company under Captain Hawkins, visited India between AD 1608 and 1611. Finch's "large journal" recording his journey was found by Rev. Samuel Purchas (1577?-1626), while searching the archives of the Company. Purchas, an English cleric, published several volumes of accounts by travellers to foreign countries under the title, *Purchas His Pilgrimage*.

While in Ayodhya, William Finch observed Hindu reverence for the city of Rama's birth. He mentioned,

> the ruines of Ranichand(s) (Ram Kot, fort of Rama) castle and houses, which the Indians acknowled(g)e for the great God, saying that he tooke flesh upon him to see the *tamasha* (show or spectacle) of the world.

7. Title page of Samuel Purchas's book, *Purchas His Pilgrimage.*

8. Title page of de Laet's book.

He noted the presence of Brahmins,

> in these ruines ... who record the names of all such Indians as wash themselves in the river running thereby...

There was a cave some two miles on the further side of the river

> where it is thought his (Rama's) ashes were buried. Hither resort many from all parts of India, which carry from hence in remembrance certaine graines of rice as blacke as gun-powder, which they say have beene reserved ever since (Foster 1921: 176).

Finch, who arrived eighty years after Babur, confirmed an active Hindu presence at the site. He made no mention of Muslims offering namaaz, raising the question whether the Masjid had been abandoned soon after its construction.

His account was liberally used by two other early travellers, Joannes de Laet and Thomas Herbert. Joannes de Laet (1581-1649), a Dutch geographer and Director of the Dutch West India Company, describing 'The Route from Agra to Jounpore,' wrote,

> ... from Cannove (Kanauj) to Lacanouw (Lucknow) is 30 cos. This is a great trading centre: thence to Oudee (an ancient city, once the seat of Pathan Kings, but now almost deserted), 50 cos. Not far from this city may be seen the ruins of the fort and palace of Ramchand, whom the Indians regard as God Most High: they say that he took on him human flesh that he might see the great *tamasha* of the world. Among these ruins live certain Bramenes who carefully note down the name of all such pilgrims as duly perform their ceremonial ablutions in the neighbouring river. They say that this custom has been kept up for many centuries. About two miles from these rivers is a cave with a narrow mouth but so spacious within and with so many ramifications that it is difficult to find one's way out again. They believe that the ashes of the god are hidden here. Pilgrims come to this place from all parts of India and after worshipping the idol take away with them some grains of charred rice as proof of their visit. This rice they believe to have been kept here for many centuries (de Laet 1928: 64-65).

Virtually alike was the account of Thomas Herbert (1606-1682), who in 1627, travelled to Persia as member of King Charles I's embassy to Shah Abbas I, and from there came to India. The narration of his journeys was published in 1634 (Butler 2012). Herbert recorded,

> ... God gave them a King, propagate from the feed of the Bramyas called Ducerat, who begat Ram, a King so famous for piety and high attempts, that to this day his name is exceedingly honoured, so that when they say Ram Rame, 'tis as if they should say, all good betide you. (Herbert 1638: 47).

Further,

SOME YEARES
TRAVELS
INTO
DIVERS PARTS OF

9. Title page of Thomas Herbert's book.

> At this Oudee or Oujea (a city in Bengala & felicitated by Ganges) are many Antick Monuments, especially memorable is the pretty old castle Ranichand built by a Bannyan Pagod of that name about 994500 yeares ago after their accompt, from which to this the Bannyans have repaired to offer here and to wash away their sins in Ganges, each of which is recorded by name by the laborious Bramyns who acquaints this Pagod with their good progressions and charitable offerings (Herbert 1638: 92).

After Finch, the next significant report on Ayodhya was by Joseph Tieffenthaler, the Austrian Jesuit (1710-1785), dismissed by Left historians as "a little known traveller" (Sahmat 2010b: 1). Even a simple Google search would reveal that Tieffenthaler was a man of many parts. A trained mathematician and astronomer, he was also one of the first European geographers to write on India. His magnum opus, *Descriptio Indiae* was an account of 22 provinces of the country with their exact geographical positions calculated by means of a simple quadrant (John 1997: 403). The work contained several maps that Tieffenthaler had himself sketched. In his introduction to *Descriptio Indiae,* Tieffenthaler wrote,

> Much has been written and many scholarly works have appeared on India, her grandeur, her religion and on the manners and customs of her inhabitants. Nevertheless this very vast country offers yet an abundance of materials to

> write. It is precisely what I have been busy in assembling in this volume – such things as I have observed with my own eyes during a span of thirty years, things I have read in Persian books treating of the geography and history of India and what I have learned in the course of conversations with persons informed in these matters. In Europe, one greedily awaits the precious merchandise from India; in sending this treatise I flatter myself to believe that it will be received with the same eagerness by the curious who will appreciate my work (Sen 1962: 84).

Tieffenthaler also prepared a large book of maps on the Ganges Basin titled *Cursus Gangae fluvi Indiae maximi ...* (1765), and several works on the flora and fauna of India. He wrote on Indian religion, arts, asceticism, Parsis, Islam, and political developments from 1757 to 1764. His vocation as a missionary influenced his writing on some of these subjects.

His linguistic equipment has been described as "extraordinary" (Sen 1962: 76). Besides his native tongue, he had a good knowledge of Latin, Italian, Spanish, French, Hindustani, Arabic, and Persian. He was among the early Europeans to learn Sanskrit. He composed a Sanskrit-Persian dictionary and wrote two books in Persian (Sen 1962: 76; John 1997: 402).

Tieffenthaler forwarded some of his works to the renowned Danish professor of medicine, Dr. Kratzenstein, and the French Orientalist, Anquetil-Duperron (1731-1805). The latter commended his contribution at the French Academy of Sciences. In 1776, Tieffenthaler sent Anquetil-Duperron three large maps showing the entire course of the Ganges and the upper and lower courses of the Ghaghara Rivers (Sen 1962: 78).

Some of the manuscripts at Copenhagen were obtained by German scholar, Johann Bernoulli, who used them for his work published in 1787. Bernoulli, a member of the Royal Academy of Sciences in Berlin and the Imperial Academy in

10. Joseph Tieffenthaler's map of the Ganges and Ghaghara rivers.

St. Petersburg "found the works of Tieffenthaler so much up to the mark that he actually undertook to translate and annotate them" (Sen 1962: 86-88; John 1997: 401-02).

Tieffenthaler, who stayed in India from 1743 till his death some four decades later, toured Awadh between 1766 and 1771. He was the first to refer to the destruction of a temple at Rama's birthplace by a Mughal ruler. He saw Hindus worshipping a religious structure in the form of a *vedi* (cradle) in the premises, but said nothing about Muslims offering namaaz. He also noted the large gatherings of Hindus on the occasion of *Rama Navami* (Rama's birthday). He wrote,

> Emperor Aurengzebe got the fortress called Ramcot demolished and got a Muslim temple, with triple domes, constructed at the same place. Others say that it was constructed by 'Babor.' Fourteen black stone pillars of 5 span high, which had existed at the site of the fortress, are seen there. Twelve of these pillars now support the interior arcades of the mosque...
>
> On the left is seen a square box raised 5 inches above the ground, with borders made of lime, with a length of more than 5 ells and a maximum width of about 4 ells. The Hindus call it Bedi i.e. 'the cradle.' The reason for this is that once upon a time, here was a house where Beschan was born in the form of Ram. ... Subsequently Aurengzebe or Babor, according to others, got this place razed in order to deny the noble people, the opportunity of practicing their superstitions. However, there still exists some superstitious cult in some place or other. For example, in the place where the native house of Ram existed, they go around 3 times and prostrate on the floor. The two spots are surrounded by a low wall constructed with battlements. One enters the front hall through a low semi-circular door .... On the 24th of the Tschet month, a big gathering of people is done here to celebrate the birthday of Ram, so famous in the entire India ... (pages 3503-09 para 3514).

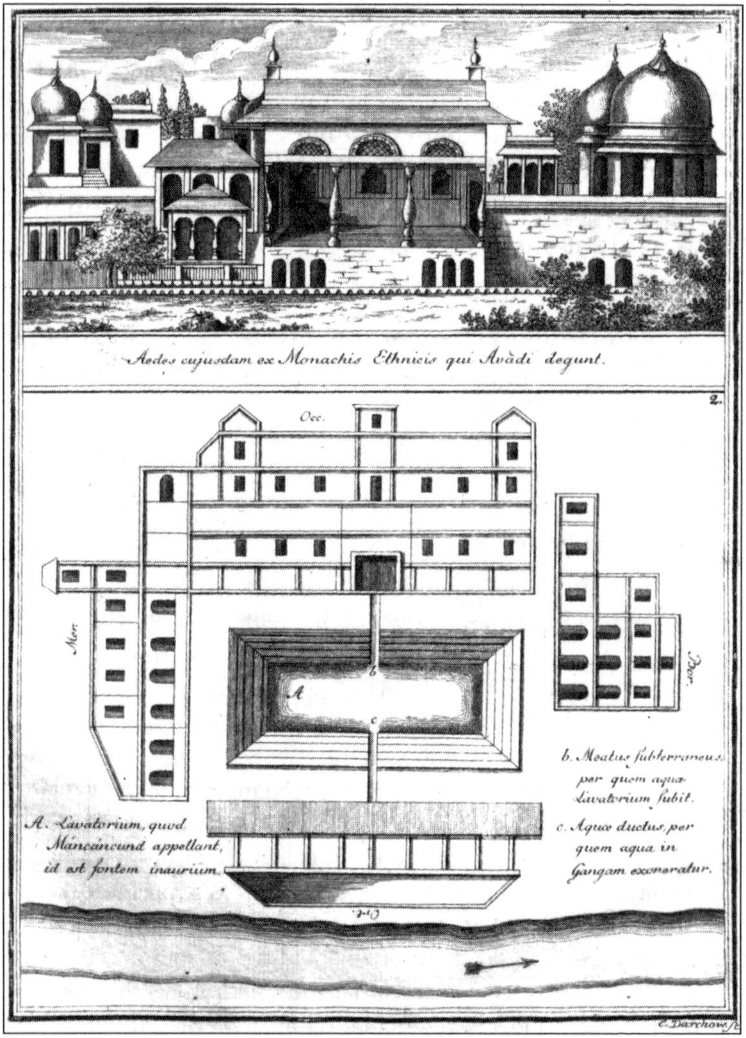

11. Sketch by Joseph Tieffenthaler.

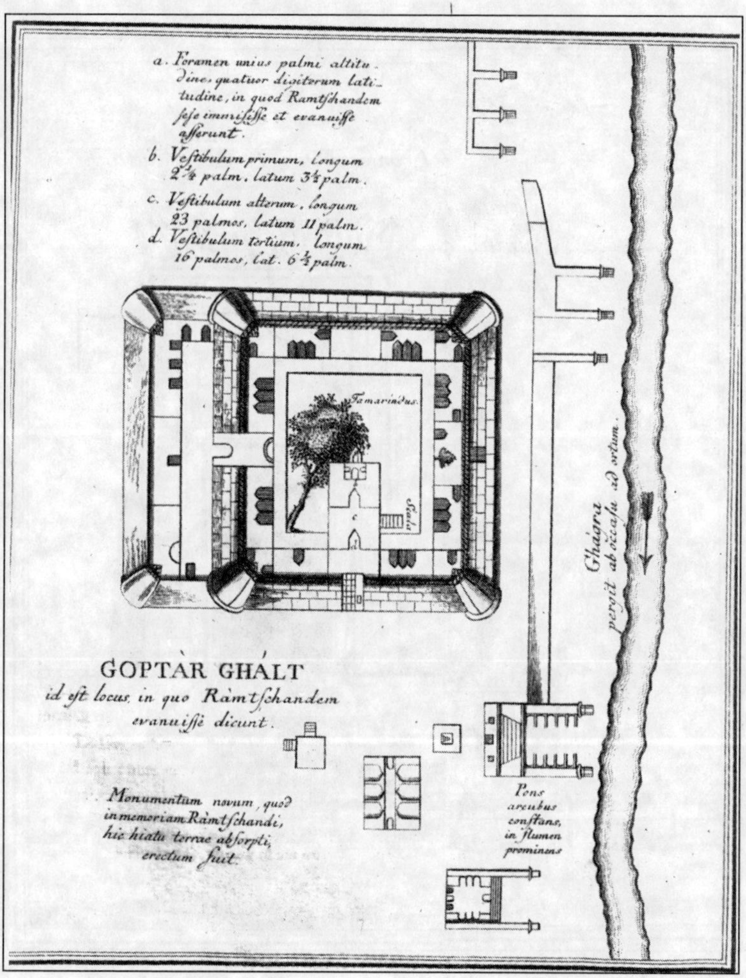

12. Sketch by Joseph Tieffenthaler.

13. Sketch by Joseph Tieffenthaler.

14. Sketch by Joseph Tieffenthaler.

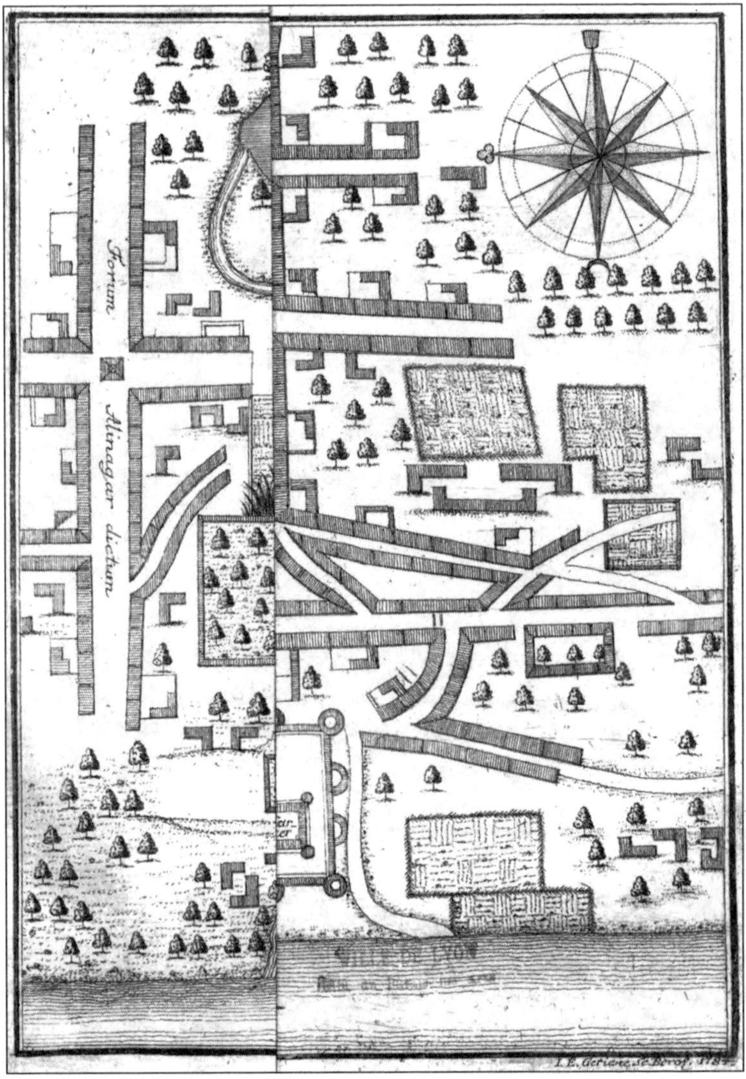

15. Sketch by Joseph Tieffenthaler.

Subsequently, Walter Hamilton, in his *Gazetteer* of 1828, also recorded the arrival of pilgrims who "resort to this vicinity, where the remains of the ancient city of Oude, and capital of the Great Rama are still to be seen." He added that religious mendicants "walk round the temples and idols, bathe in the holy pools, and perform the customary ceremonies" (Hamilton I 1828: 350).

The British official, Robert Montgomery Martin, entrusted in 1838, with the task of compiling historical and topographical data on Eastern India (collected earlier by Francis Buchanan), reported the legend of King Vikramaditya who allegedly erected 360 temples at places sanctified by the deeds of Rama, Sita, Lakshmana, and Hanuman. He referred to the destruction of the temple by Babur or Aurangzeb. "The bigot, by whom the temples were destroyed, is said to have erected mosques on the situations of the most remarkable temples." Martin mentioned the black stone pillars in the mosque, evidently taken from a Hindu building from the traces of images observable on some of their bases, though these had been cut off "to satisfy the conscience of the bigot" (Martin II 1838: 333-36).

Edward Thornton (1799-1875), head of the Statistical Department of East India House and pioneer in the systematic collection and publication of Indian statistics, in his Gazetteer of 1858 wrote that the mosque was embellished with fourteen columns,

> said to have been taken from the ruins of the Hindoo fanes...A quadrangular coffer of stone, white washed, five ells long, four broad, and protruding five or six inches above ground, is pointed out as the cradle in which Rama was born as the seventh avatar of Vishnu; and is accordingly abundantly honoured by the pilgrimages and devotions of the Hindoos (Thornton 1858: 739-40).

Surgeon General Edward Balfour (1813-1889), Scottish surgeon, Orientalist, and environmentalist, in the *Encyclopaedia of Indian and of Eastern and Southern Asia* stated that Ayodhya had "three mosques on the sites of three Hindu shrines: the Janmasthan on the site where Rama was born ..." (Balfour 1858: 56).

Patrick Carnegy, the first British Commissioner and Settlement Officer of Faizabad wrote,

> It is locally affirmed that at the Mahomedan conquest there were three important Hindu shrines ... at Ayodhya. These were the Janmasthan, the Sargadwar Mandir and the Treta-ka-Thakur. On the first of these Babar built the mosque which still bears his name... On the second, Aurangzeb did the same ... and on the third that sovereign, or his predecessor, built a mosque, according to the well-known Mahomedan principle of enforcing their religion on all whom they conquered (Carnegy 1870: 20-21).

Carnegy stated that the Janmasthan marked the place where Rama was born, the Sargadwar the gate through which he passed into heaven and the Treta-ka-Thakur the site where he performed a great sacrifice.

W.C. Benett, who prepared the *Gazetteer of the Province of Oudh* (1877-78), noted,

> If Ajodhya was then little other than a wilderness, it must at least have possessed a fine temple in the Janamasthan; for many of its columns are still in existence and in good preservation, having been used by the Musalmans in the construction of the Babari Mosque. These are of strong, close-grained, dark-colored or black stone, called by the natives *kasauti* and carved with different devices (Benett 1877-78: 6-7).[1]

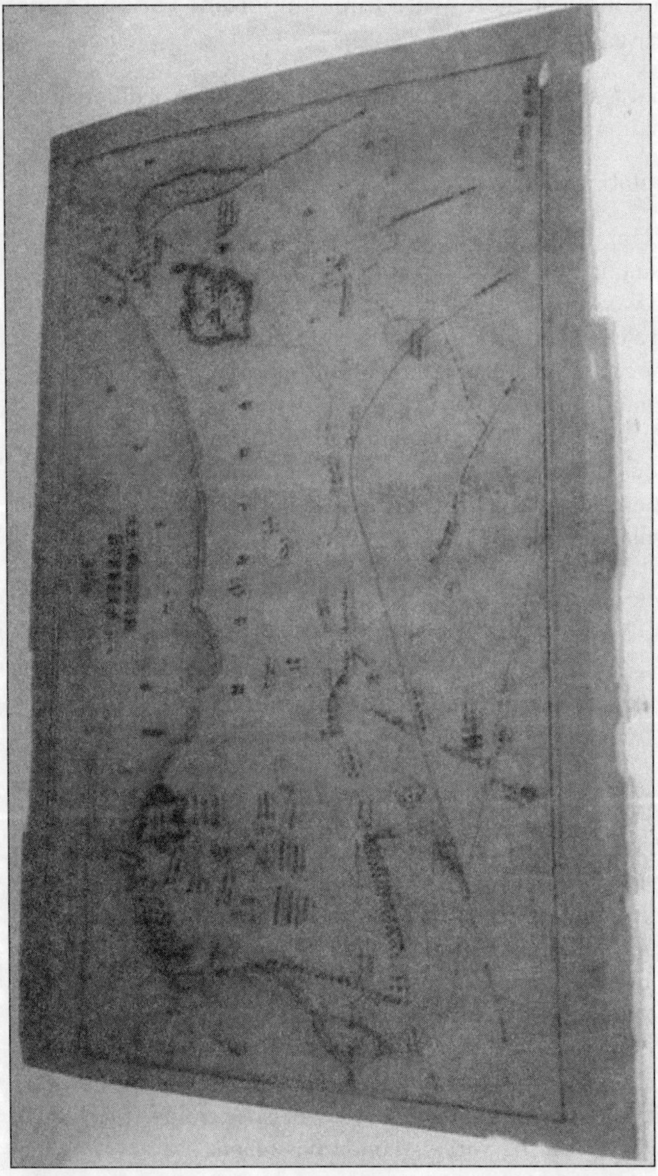

16. Patrick Carnegy's map of Ayodhya, 1870.

H.R. Nevill (ICS) also recorded that at the time of the Muslim conquest there were three important Hindu shrines at Ayodhya,

> each was successively made the object of attention of different Musalman rulers.

He elaborated,

> The Janmasthan was in Ramkot and marked the birthplace of Ram. In AD 1528 Babar came to Ajodhya and halted there for a week. He destroyed the ancient temple and on its site built a mosque, still known as Babar's mosque. The materials of the old structure were largely employed, and many of the columns are in good preservation; they are of close-grained black stone, called by the natives *kasauti*, and carved with various devices ... This desecration of the most sacred spot in the city caused great bitterness between Hindus and Musalmans (Nevill 1905: 179-80).

Alexander Cunningham, the leading British archaeologist of India in the nineteenth century, in his Report of 1862-1863, wrote, "...in the very heart of the city stands the Janam Asthan, or 'Birth-place temple' of Rama" (Cunningham I 1871: 322).

END NOTES

1. Well after independence, the *UP District Gazetteers – Faizabad* (1960), also recorded,
   The Janmasthan was in Ramkot and marked the birthplace of Rama. It seems that in AD 1528 Babur visited Ayodhya and under his orders this ancient temple was destroyed and on the site was built what came to be known as Babur's mosque. The material of the old temple was largely employed in building the mosque and a few of the original columns are still in good preservation; they are of close grained black stone (*kasauti*) bearing various Hindu bas-reliefs...

Subsequently Aurangzeb also desecrated the shrines of Ayodhya which led to prolonged bitterness between the Hindus and Muslims. The latter occupied the Janmasthan by force and also made an assault on Hanuman Garhi....As a result, in 1858 an outer enclosure was put up in front of the mosque and the Hindus, who were forbidden access to the inner yard, had to perform their puja on a platform outside...Outside the outer wall of this contested shrine there is an old and broken image of the Varah (boar) (Joshi 1960: 352-53).

4

Attempts to Reclaim Sacred Spaces

Many of the sacred centres of Hinduism suffered grievously under the Turkish onslaught. Banaras, Mathura, Ayodhya ...[1]

In Banaras, the Krittivasa, Omkara, Mahadeva, Madhyameshvara, Vishvanath, Bindu Madhava, and Kaal Bhairava temples were all razed. In many cases, mosques were built with "calculated insolence" in their place and the sites closed to Hindus (Lannoy 1999: 569). Other holy cities met a similar fate. The British District Commissioner, F.S. Growse noted that in Mathura as a consequence of "Muhammadan intolerance" not a single structure of antiquity had survived (Growse 1882: 126).

There was no perceptible improvement during the subsequent centuries of the Delhi Sultans. In Braj, only two pre-Mughal Hindu monuments are still standing, the Assi Khambha at Mahaban and the Chaurasi Khambha at Kaman; still standing because they were refashioned into mosques. Everything else, Buddhist, Jain, Hindu was abandoned and left to collapse, or destroyed (Entwistle 1987: 134).

17. A drawing of the Kashi Vishvanath temple after its demolition, by James Prinsep in 1826.

SOUTH INDIA

In South India, a sense of cultural loss was depicted in several works, among them the *Madhuravijaya*, a fourteenth century Sanskrit poem by Gangadevi, wife of Prince Kampana of Vijayanagar,

> In the temples which once resounded with the joyous music of the mridana, there is heard at present only the howl of the jackals that have made them their abode...The river Tamraparni which used to be rendered white by the sandal paste, rubbed away from the breasts of youthful maidens at their bath, is now flowing red with the blood of the slaughtered cows (*Madhura Vijaya* 1924: 5-7)

A fresh group of defenders came to the fore, pre-eminent among them Prince Kampana, Vishnu incarnate, anointed by the Goddess herself as the true successor of the Pandya kings. Kampana was the restorer of *dharma*, the benefactor of countless temples in the Tamil land, several of which had been converted into mosques (Davis 2015: 119-22).

The flight of Sri Rangathana from the Ranganatha temple due to the arrival of the army of the Delhi Sultan was recorded in several medieval accounts. The *Koyil Oluku* detailed the fifty-nine year long endeavour to recover the image of the main processional deity. The *Tirunarayanapura,* another variant of the event, highlighted the role of the saint Ramanuja in the retrieval of the Ramapriya statue and its installation in the Tirunarayanapura temple. Anantasuri's *Prapannamrta*, written three centuries after the event, demonstrated a vivid popular memory of the incident (Davis 2015: 129-37).

THE CASE OF BRAJ

Gradually, Hindus attempted to reoccupy their sacred sites. In Braj, holy places associated with the life of Krishna were steadily reclaimed by the saints Nimbarka (a Tailang Brahmin from Andhra who lived in the thirteenth century), Vallabha (a Tailang Brahmin born in the forest of Champa, Madhya Pradesh in 1479), Chaitanya (born in 1486 in the town of Nabadwip, in Bengal), and their many disciples. A saint, Madhavendra Puri was credited with establishing an image of Krishna at Govardhan in the fifteenth century (Vaudeville 2005: 55-57; Entwistle 1987: 136-44).

In 1552, Narayan Bhatt compiled the *Vrajabhaktivilasa*, the most comprehensive list of the sacred places of Braj (Entwistle 1987: 149). Akbar's Rajput mansabdars contributed significantly to the restoration of Hindu pilgrimage sites. Many new temples were built, with the same red sandstone used in the imperial buildings at Agra and Fatehpur Sikri. The Jesuit, Father Monserrate, who stayed at Akbar's çourt for two years beginning in 1580, on a visit to Mathura, noted that temples of Krishna "elegantly built in the pyramidal style," were found at several places associated with the Lord's exploits. He saw the ruins of earlier buildings;

> only one Hindu temple is left out of many; for the Musalmans have completely destroyed all except the pyramids. Huge crowds of pilgrims come from all over India to this temple, which is situated on the high bank of the Jomanis (Entwistle 1987: 157-58).

Jahangir, like Akbar, visited the area around Mathura for tiger hunting. His only recorded comment was that he found it difficult to breathe inside the temples in Vrindavan because of the presence of numerous bats,

> After marching four stages from this halting-place, the army of prosperity encamped outside Mathura. On Thursday, the 8th, I went to see Brindaban and the idol temples of that place.
>
> Although in the time of the late king the Rajput nobles had built temples after their fashion, and ornamented them highly on the outside, inside them bats and owls had made their abode to such an extent, that on account of their odours one could not breathe (*Tuzuk-i-Jahangiri* II 1914: 103-05).

18. A photograph of the back side of the Gyanwapi mosque which rests on part of the Kashi Vishvanath temple.

Things again became difficult thereafter. In 1632, Emperor Shah Jahan forbade the completion of all temples begun in the time of Jahangir, and ordered the destruction of those at Varanasi, Allahabad, Orchha, Kashmir, and Gujarat.

The Keshavdev temple, seen by the French travellers Francois Bernier in 1663 and Jean-Baptiste Tavernier in 1650,

19. The Madanmohan temple, Vrindavan as published in F.S. Growse's *Mathura: A District Memoir*, 1882.

20. The Gobind Dev temple converted into a mosque. The *mehrab* is visible on top.

was razed to the ground in 1669 following Aurangzeb's orders to demolish Hindu shrines. An idgah was constructed at the site.

Aurangzeb's policies prompted an exodus of deities from Braj. The deities of the Gobind Dev, Gopinath, Madanmohan, Radhavallabh temples all left. The custodians of Shrinathji also decided to remove the deity from the Govardhan temple. The *Sri Nathji ki Prakatya Varta* recorded the Lord's journey after leaving the temple; first to Agra, then Kota, later to Kishangarh; then on the way to Udaipur, the Lord's cart got stuck at the village of Sinhad, 40 km from the city. The deity was installed in a hastily constructed shrine, later replaced by a larger temple. The journey from Govardhan to Sinhad had taken two years, four months, and seven days (Peabody 1991: 727; Entwistle 1987: 157-58).

Unlike the image of Srinathji, which is three-fifths life-size, other images of the Vallabha Sampradaya are only a few centimeters tall. These often escaped "the iconoclastic Mughal horde" by being concealed in the turbans of temple servants. The events were encapsulated in a code phrase of the Vallabha Sampradaya, "In whose turban does the Lord reside?" (Peabody 1991: 728).

The image of Gobind Dev (installed in the Gobind Dev temple at Vrindavan by Raja Man Singh of Amer in 1590) was also removed in 1669.[2] After a long journey, the image was eventually installed in a temple within the precincts of Sawai Jai Singh's palace in Jaipur, in 1739 (Okita 2014: 27-29). The gesture has been interpreted as marking the "growing assertiveness" of the Rajputs in the time of Mughal decline (Horstmann 1999a: 8).

Meanwhile, in Braj, devotional activity did not come to a complete standstill. Pilgrimage declined, but had picked up by the time Sawai Jai Singh was appointed Governor of Agra in 1722.

MARATHA INITIATIVES

As the Mughal Empire declined, the Marathas were foremost among the rulers to attempt to reclaim Hindu sacred sites. On 18th June 1751, a Maratha agent reported,

> Malharrao (Holkar) has pitched his monsoon camp in the Doab. He intended to pull down the grand Masjid built by Aurangzeb at Benares and restore the original temple of Kashi-Vishveshwar. The Brahmans of Kashi feel extremely terrified at such a move, for they realize the Muslim strength in these places (Sardesai 1958: 377).

Balaji Baji Rao, the Peshwa, gave considerable attention to the repossession of Hindu holy sites. In a letter to Ramaji Anant, the manager of Sindhia, on 23rd February 1759, he directed,

> Take Benares, Ajodhya and Allahabad from him (Shuja-ud-daulah, the third Nawab of Awadh, 1754-1775). He had promised to Dada (Raghunath Rao in 1757) to cede Benares and Ajodhya, but the case of Allahabad is still under discussion. If a settlement on the last point can be easily reached, make it (Sarkar II 1966: 161).

Writing to Dattaji and Jankoji Sindhia on 21st March 1759, the Peshwa further instructed,

> If he (Shuja-ud-daulah) is now made wazir (by us), he must cede both Benares and Allahabad and pay 50 *lakhs*. If he refuses to make the above territorial surrenders and asks for 2 or 3 years to complete the payment (of 50 *lakhs*), do not give him the wazirship. But give it if he pays 50 *lakhs* and at least Allahabad ... (Sarkar 1966 II: 162-63).

In his will of AD 1772, Peshwa Madhav Rao (r. 1761-1772) also exhorted his successors to get hold of Prayag and Banaras. "This was the ardent desire of my sires," read his final testament, "and now is the time to carry it out" (Sardesai 1958: 558).

In the eighteenth century, Banaras was also substantially rebuilt with generous Maratha contribution (Altekar 1947: 247). Among the temples they constructed were those of Annapurna, Kaal Bhairava, Sakshivinayaka, Trilochanesvara, and the Vishvanath Ghat (Eck 1983).

SAWAI JAI SINGH

By the time of Aurangzeb's death, the Amer ruler, Sawai Jai Singh (r. 1700-1743) had emerged among the leading princes of North India. Letters from the rulers of Marwar, Kota, Narwar, and Chhatra Sal of Mahoba, preserved at Jaipur described him as "the head and crown of all Hindustan," and "the protector of all Hindustan" (Sarkar 1984: 223-24).

The *jizya*, abolished by Emperor Farrukh Siyar in January 1713, had been re-imposed in April 1717. Jai Singh used his position to appeal against the tax with Emperor Muhammad Shah. In 1728, on his advice, the tax on pilgrims at Gaya was abolished, and in 1730, again at his intercession, the tax on Hindus at certain bathing sites was also withdrawn (Sarkar 1984: 224-26). Jai Singh strove to improve conditions for pilgrims in Hindu holy cities. In 1733, he secured the *faujdari* of Gaya, in addition to that he held of Mathura, which enabled him to contribute to the uplift of holy sites in the region (Bhatnagar 1974: 340-41).

Jai Singh visualized the revival of Hindu glory in collaboration with the Rajputs and Marathas; he helped the latter to establish themselves in Malwa. In a letter, dated 26th October 1731, to Nandlal Mandloi of Indore, Jai Singh wrote,

> Thousand praises to you that, at my word alone you and the rest of the sardars protected our religion in Malwa by driving out the Muhammadans from there. You have fulfilled my desire. In return for this I have written to the Peshwa to arrange the affairs of all the sardars of Malwa according to your wishes (Sinha 1954: 150).

In a bid to project himself as the perfect Hindu king, Jai Singh invoked the great symbols of Hindu tradition (Horstmann 2011: 75; Okita 2014: 30-35). He revived and performed several Vedic sacrifices and also attempted to assimilate the various Vaishnava *bhakti* orders (Horstmann 2002: 159). In 1708, he performed the *vajapeya yajna*, a ceremony linked to claims to universal kingship. The *yajna*, performed annually when he was engaged in a struggle with the Mughals, was indicative of the role he wished to carve out for himself. Jai Singh twice commissioned the *asvamedha yajna*, first in 1734, and then again in 1741. The revival of the *yajna*, customarily an announcement of unchallenged sovereignty, after a hiatus of over seven centuries, was regarded a historic event. Scholars at Varanasi, declared, "If the *Yajna* was not performed after Janmejay, the reason was that after him, no king was born who had enough confidence and who could turn victorious in all directions." Towards the end of his life, Jai Singh also performed the *rajsuya yajna*, but died before its completion (Bhatt 2005: 139, 136).

The militant Ramanandis enjoyed a special relationship with the Jaipur state. Lord Rama was regarded the forerunner of the dynasty. To become ruler, the king had to be initiated with the Rama *mantra* by a Ramanandi *Mahant* (Horstmann 2011: 80).

The Ramanandis were represented in the eighteenth century by two lineages, those of Galata and Ravasa (Ghurye 1964: 166-67). In the first quarter of the century, a conference of the Ramanandi *sampradaya* was held at Galata, near Jaipur, under the auspices of Sawai Jai Singh. At this conference, the head of the Ramanandis, Balananda, was entrusted the responsibility of organizing military wings (*naga* sections) of the various Vaishnava sects. Govindadas (of the Nirmohi *akhara*) established the first *akhara* of the Ramanandis in Ayodhya soon after his arrival from the Conference. Around the same time, Abhayramadas founded the Nirvani *akhara* on Hanuman Tila. Gradually, in the course of the century, all other Ramanandi *akharas* established themselves in Ayodhya. Some old structures already existing in the city were repaired and restored by them (Ghurye 1964: 178-79; Veer 1989: 98-101; 137-45; Burghart 2005: 227-49).

The changing political equations following the death of Aurangzeb would have facilitated these developments. In 1714, within seven years of Aurangzeb's death, Emperor Farrukhsiyar appointed Chhabile Ram Governor of Awadh, where he served for almost a year. In 1720, the Sayyid Brothers assigned the same post to Girdhar Bahadur; who remained in office till 1722. Perhaps, circumambulation around the *vedi* (noticed by Tieffenthaler), and worship inside the mosque (later recorded by Patrick Carnegy) began around this time (Kunal 2016: 360, 386-87). The shift of the Nawabi court from

Ayodhya to Faizabad in the time of the second Nawab of Awadh, Safdar Jung (1739-1754), would have hastened changes (Bakker 1991: 91). In 1739, Safdar Jang selected Newal Ray as Naib (Deputy) of Awadh. Ray continued in that post till his death in 1751. The construction of several buildings along the Svarga Dwara in Ayodhya is credited to him. In 1757, Nawab Shuja ud-Daula (1754-1775) selected Beni Bahadur for that office, where he served till 1767 (Fisher 1987: 55-56, 250).

JAISINGHPURAS

Jai Singh founded several small, fortified townships or localities, called *Jaisinghpuras,* at places where he was posted, for instance at Kabul, Peshawar, Multan, Lahore, Delhi, Agra, Patna, Burhanpur, Aurangabad, and Ellichpur. He also purchased land and established *Jaisinghpuras* at important Hindu religious centres in northern India, such as Mathura, Vrindavan, Kashi-Banaras, Prayaga-Allahabad, Ujjain, and Ayodhya, in a bid to restore Hindu *Dharma* (Bhatt 2005: 145).

The Kapad-Dwar collection of the SMS-II City Palace Museum at Jaipur contains several documents linked to the Ayodhya dispute. Professor R. Nath examined a large number of *pattas, parwanas, chak-namas,* letters, and other documents and maps preserved in this collection. These showed that the Rama Janmasthan was situated in *Jaisinghpura,* the land of which had been acquired by Sawai Jai Singh in perpetuity in AD 1717. The ownership of the Rama Janmasthan land was vested in the deity. According to Professor Nath, the hereditary title of ownership of the Kachhwahas of Amer-Jaipur was recognized and enforced by the Mughal State from AD 1717, when the grant was originally made (Nath 1993a).

It is pertinent to recall that in 1723, Mughal Emperor Muhammad Shah renewed the grant of six *bighas* of land to Hanuman Tila made by Akbar in 1600. He also abolished the *jaziya,* and gifted land to a *matha* at Bodh Gaya. This could be indicative of the changing power equations following the death of Aurangzeb.

The impact of the new political reality was felt instantaneously in Ayodhya. A letter written to Sawai Jai Singh by a *gumashta*, Tilokchand, dated v. 1780 (AD 1723) recorded that a *mela* (fair) was to be held at the Janmasthan,

> Tilokchand has the honour of submitting this document, dated Kartik 7, Samvat 1780, before Maharaja Shri Sawai Jaisinghji to inform that the fair of Nanwar Tirth is to be held on Assauj 10 at Jaisinghpura ... Earlier under the rule of Mlechhas, the people had to bathe secretly. Now, since Jaisinghpura has been established, all the people of Ayodhya will be coming for (the holy) bath on the auspicious day (Nath 1993a).

MAPS

The Kapad Dwar collection at SMS-II City Palace Museum also has at least eight maps of Ayodhya; five being parts of a large map showing Ayodhya and its neighbourhood. They can be assigned to the first quarter of the eighteenth century (1710-1725). The sixth map, measuring 83.5 x 83.5 cm is a religious map of Ayodhya of the same period. Two other maps preserved in the collection are particularly important. One measuring 101 x 62.2 cm painted in red, green, and yellow on paper pasted on white cotton cloth, provides a panoramic view of Ayodhya. It was prepared in accordance with the prevailing system of cartography. Place names are written in Nagari and among the various *kunds*, temples and other religious places, the temple of Sri Rama is also discretely marked.

Another map, measuring 213 x 178 cm and titled *Ayodhya kila aur kasba* (Ayodhya Fort and Town), is painted on white cotton cloth. It depicts along with palaces, *kunds,* and other religious places, the structure of Janmasthan at the corner of the Ram Kot, the enclosing ramparts of which are clearly shown. The open court occupies more space than the built structure, on one side of which is a *chabutra* (raised platform). Figures dressed in typical eighteenth century style are shown circumambulating and worshipping it. The main building is divided into three bays, each containing a *chowki* with *masand*. The central one is marked *chhathi*, which also denotes a birthplace (Nath 1993b). The courtyard in the middle of the map has *'janmasthan'* written on it. It is unclear whether the cartographer wanted to indicate a building or a spot in the courtyard. Although the marking was outside the three-domed building depicted in the map, so were the markings of other structures on it (Nath 1993b; Nath 2004: 39-46).

END NOTES

1. In a memorable passage, Al-Biruni described the Turkish advent and the havoc it caused,

   Now in the following times no Muslim conqueror passed beyond the frontier of Kabul and the river Sindh until the days of the Turks, when they seized the power in Ghazna under the Samani dynasty, and the supreme power fell to the lot of Nasir-addaula Sabuktagin. This prince chose the holy war as his calling, and therefore called himself Al-ghazi (i.e. warring on the road of Allah). In the interest of his successors he constructed, in order to weaken the Indian frontier, those roads on which afterwards his son Yamin-addaula Mahmud marched into India during a period of thirty years and more. God be merciful to both father and son! Mahmud utterly ruined the prosperity of the country, and performed there wonderful exploits, by which the Hindus became like atoms of dust scattered in all directions, and like a tale of old in the mouth of the people. Their scattered remains cherish, of course, the most inveterate aversion towards the Muslims. This is the reason, too, why Hindu sciences have retired far away from those parts of the country conquered by us, and have fled to places which our hand cannot yet reach, to Kashmir, Benares, and other places. And there the antagonism between them and all foreigners receives more and more nourishment both from political and religious sources (Sachau 1888: 22).

2. The upper part of the temple was destroyed on Aurangzeb's orders prior to his intended visit in 1670. On top of the ruin, a mosque (a *mehrab* or prayer hall) was erected, where Aurangzeb is believed to have offered *namaaz*. The mosque can clearly be seen on top of the temple in a picture published in *Mathura, a District Gazetteer*. The British District Commissioner, F. S. Growse ordered the removal of the mosque and restored the temple to the Vaishnavas in 1871.

5

Muslim Sources on Ramjanmabhumi/Babri Masjid

Several works in Arabic, Persian, and Urdu discussed the demolition of the Ramjanmabhumi temple and its replacement by Babri Masjid (Narain 1993: 16-37). Among them was the *Jannah al-Mashriq wa Matla 'an-Nur al-Mashriq*, re-titled *Al-Hind-u fi al- 'Ahd al-Islami*, by Maulana Hakim Sayyid Abd al-Hayy. It was translated into Urdu by Maulana Shams Tabriz Khan, under the title *Hindustan Islami Ahd mein*. In an introduction, the author's son, Maulana Abu l-Hasan 'Ali Nadawi alias Ali Mian, wrote,

> And among them is the great mosque that was built by the Timurid king Babar in the sacred city of Ajodhya. It is believed that Rama Chandra considered to be the manifestation of God, was born here. There is a long story about his wife Sita. There was a big temple for them in this city. At a certain place Sita used to sit and cook food for her consort. Well, the said king Babar demolished it and built a mosque at that very place with chiseled stone in 923 AH (Narain 1993: 16-17).

Another work was the *Hadiqah-i Shuhada,* (Lucknow 1856), by Mirza Jan, a participant in the *jihad* of Amir Ali at Hanuman Garhi in 1855. Mirza Jan referred to a Persian text, *Sahifah-i Chihal Nasaih-I Bahadurshahi* (*the Bahadurshahi Book of Forty Sermons*), attributed to a granddaughter of Emperor Aurangzeb. He claimed to have found a copy of the book, made on 11th July 1816, in the library of the grandson of Prince Dara Shukoh. Among its sermons, the book advised devout Muslim rulers to keep idolaters in subjection to Islam and,

> keep in constant use for Friday and congregational prayer the mosques built up to strengthen Islam after demolishing the temples of the idolatrous Hindus situated at Mathura, Banaras, and Awadh etc., which the wretched infidels have, according to their faith, adjudged to be the birthplace of Krishna in one case, Sita ki Rasoi in another, and Hanuman's abode in a third ...

The authenticity and authorship of this work is debatable (Kunal 2016: 253-57). Mirza Jan did not name the daughter of Bahadur Shah, nor cite the year in which she composed this work. However, according to the Foreign Department Political Consultations, December 28, 1855, No. 450, the Prime Minister of Nawab Wajid Ali Shah of Awadh "referred to a book which existed in the King's library written in the reign of Bahadurshah about the year AD 1707 which contained an account of the Masjid at Hanumangarhi." While quoting from the above text, Mirza Jan remarked,

> In short, these four mosques (Babri mosque, Ram Darbar mosque, Fort mosque, and Hanumanagadhi mosque) built by the rulers of the past were situated at Ayodhya like four pillars of the faith (Narain 1993: 23-26).

In his *Hadiqah-i Shuhada,* Mirza Jan wrote,

> ...they (Muslim rulers) cleared up Faizabad and Awadh also from the filth of false belief, inasmuch as it is a great place of

> worship and was the capital of Rama's father. Here they broke the temples and left no stone-hearted idol intact. Where there was a big temple, there they got a big mosque constructed, and, where there was a small pavilion, there they erected a plain camp mosque/enclosure. Accordingly, what a majestic mosque Babar Shah has got constructed in 923 AH under the patronage of Sayyid Musa Ashiqan! Its date is "*Khayr Baqi.*" It is still known far and wide as the *Sita ki Rasoi* mosque (Narain 1993: 35-36).

Several other works in Urdu written in the nineteenth and early twentieth century also referred to the replacement of the temple by the mosque. The *Tarikh-i Awadh* (1919), for instance, stated,

> Babur got the mosque built after demolishing the Janmasthan and used in his mosque the stone of the same Janmasthan, which was richly engraved, precious *kasauti* stone, and which survives even today.

The *Qaysar-u't Tawarikh* located the mosque in Sita ki Rasoi as well as the Janmasthan. It acknowledged, "...all the temples of Ayodhya were turned into mosques by the Sultans of the past" (Narain 1993: 27-35).

The *Fasanah-I Ibrat,* written by Rajab Ali Beg Surur in 1860, but first published in 1884, stated,

> ...a glorious mosque was built up during King Babar's regime on the spot where Sita ki Rasoi tomb (?) is situated in Awadh. During this Babari (dispensation) the Hindus had no guts to be a match for the Muslims. (The mosque) was built in 923 AH under the patronage of Sayyid Mir Ashiqan ... There (on Hanumangadhi) Aurangzib constructed a mosque ... The Bairagis effaced the mosque and erected a temple in its place. Then they intruded into the 'Masjid-I Babari' where the Sita ki Rasoi was situated (Narain 1993: 30).

Muraqqah-i Khusrawi, or the *Tawarikh-i Awadh,* by Shaykh Azamat Ali Kakorawi Nami (1811-1893), an eye witness to several events of the reign of Nawab Wajid Ali Shah, was completed in 1869 but published in 1986. The manuscript is preserved at the Tagore Library, University of Lucknow. The parts dealing with the construction of Babri Masjid and the Hindu-Muslim conflict of 1855 were deleted by the Fakhruddin Ahmad Memorial Committee, under whose auspices the book was published. Zakir Kakaurwi published these sections separately under the title *Amir Ali Shahid Aur Marakhai-i-Hanuman Garhi* in 1987 (Grover and Gupta 1991: 152). It stated,

> According to old records, it has been a religious rule with Muslim rulers, after the triumph of Sayyid Salar Masud Ghazi, to build mosques, monasteries, and inns, spread Islam, and put a stop to blasphemous practices (bid at), wherever they found manifestation (of infidelity). Accordingly, even as they cleared up Mathura, Bindraban, etc. from the rubbish of non-Islamic practices, the magnificent Babari mosque (*masjid-I sarbaland-i Babari*) came up in 923 AH under the patronage of Sayyid Musa Ashiqan in the Janmasthan temple (*butkhane Janmasthan mein*) in Faizabad-Awadh which was a great place (of idol-worship) and the capital of Rama's father... Among the Hindus it was known as Sita ki Rasoi (Narain 1993: 29-30).

A translation of the same work provided by Kishore Kunal affirmed that Hindus had begun worship at Babri Masjid and officials kept quiet after accepting bribes,

> Then in the Baburi mosque, where there was Sita Rasoi, started the worship openly. Officers, after taking bribes (silver shoes), became their loyal servants. No one took notice. First the saying of Shaikh Ali Haji was true to the situation – 'The *butkhana* on the way that was considered a bad place became the abode of God!'
>
> Thereafter, a drastic change occurred – mosques were pulled down and temples were constructed there. But there was a

> veil of neglect on our eyes and we remained in slumber (Kunal 2016: 259-60).

The *Tarikh -i- Awadh (Ḥissa Doyam)* by Allama Muhammad Nazamul Gani Khan Rampuri (1859-1932) stated,

> .... At last, the tussle went to such an extent that except the mosque adjacent to Hanuman-garhi, the Hindus made Butkhana even in the corridor of the Babri mosque where existed Sita Rasoi. The Hindus damaged Ram Ghat mosque also and in its corridor constructed a temple. They started placing garbage in the mosque and constructed magnificent temple from the bricks and stones after digging hundreds of graves of the Muslims (Kunal 2016: 260-61).

Perhaps this described the situation after the Galata conference when the Ramanandis began arriving in Ayodhya in considerable numbers.

Professor Irfan Habib dismissed these works as the product of the communal consciousness of the last 150 years (*Muslim India* 101, May 1991). It would have contributed immensely to the debate had Professor Habib listed Arabic, Persian, Urdu, Hindavi, Hindustani, or Hindi works that asserted that Babri Masjid was built on virgin land.

In addition to the works listed by Harsh Narain, B.R. Grover and S.P. Gupta mentioned the *Gumghasta Halat-i-Ajodhaya Awadh* (The forgotten events of Ajodhaya Awadh), by Maulvi Abdul Karim, Imam of Babri Masjid. He cited several contemporary sources in his book. It was translated from Persian to Urdu in 1979 by his grandson, Maulvi Abdul Gufar; who retained the section pertaining to the destruction of the Janmasthan temple and the construction of a mosque in its place. The revised second Urdu edition published in 1981, however, omitted this portion (Grover and Gupta 1991: 152).

6

The Conflict at Ayodhya Documented

The earliest reference to the dispute at Ayodhya found so far in the judicial records is a note submitted to the Faizabad Court in 1822 by Hafizullah, a Court official. It stated that "the mosque constructed by Babur was situated at the birth-place of Ram, son of Raja Dashrath, and was adjacent to the kitchen of Sita, wife of Ram (i.e. Sita Ki Rasoi)" (Grover 2015: 236).

THE CONFLICT OF 1855 AT HANUMAN GARHI AND JANAMASTHAN

On 8th Feb 1855, the British Resident, James Outram, sent a letter to Wajid Ali Shah, Nawab of Awadh (1847-1856),[1] cautioning him that a Sunni troublemaker Shah Ghulam Husain, had assembled a "large force" of Muslims near Faizabad, and was,

> determined to destroy and ruin the Hunuman Ghurrie which is inhabited by Hindoos and is peculiarly sacred in their estimation, his lieutenant called Moulavee Saheb is even still more diabolically inclined and ready for strife...

A large number of Hindus had assembled to defend their temple. The Resident foresaw bloodshed and urged the king to send a "very swift Camel Messenger with all possible speed," to have Shah Ghulam Husain arrested, and the situation defused (Foreign Political Consultations, 28 Dec 1855, Nos. 339-46). The king failed to act and a clash took place (Llewellyn-Jones 2015: 110-12).

This was followed by a more serious encounter in July 1855. Shah Ghulam Husian and Maulvi Muhammad Shah insisted on the right to offer prayers at a masjid supposedly inside Hanuman Garhi. The matter was reported to Wajid Ali Shah, who directed the Nazim of Sultanpur and the Kotwal of Ayodhya to investigate. However, a regular conflict broke out when the Muslims tried to enter Hanuman Garhi; they were beaten back by the Bairagis and suffered a loss of over seventy lives (Bhatnagar 1968: 117-18).

On 11th August 1855, the British Resident forwarded to the Nawab two bonds he had secured from Bairagis, Mahants Balran Dass, Kishen Dass, Bansi Dass, and Debi Ram, the previous day. In the first bond, the Mahants declared,

> Whereas Gholam Husein and others have laid a claim to a musjid in Hunooman Gurhee, and have caused a collision with us on that account and whereas Jafir Alee and Kurum Khan and others of Oude, have become aggrieved and angry with us, as they joined with Gholam Husein; therefore, having in view our former friendship and acquaintance, we declare we have no enmity towards them and agreeing to Agha Alee Khan, Raja Maun Singh and Captain Orr, as our arbitrators, we solemnly swear by Mahabeer and hereby write, that we will not on any account create any disturbance, or tumult, on condition that no one molests us, or abuses us. All the Byragees who are of our tribe will not do anything contrary to what we have written, and as formerly we treated Jafir Alee and others, so we will now be friendly with them. If we act contrary to what we have

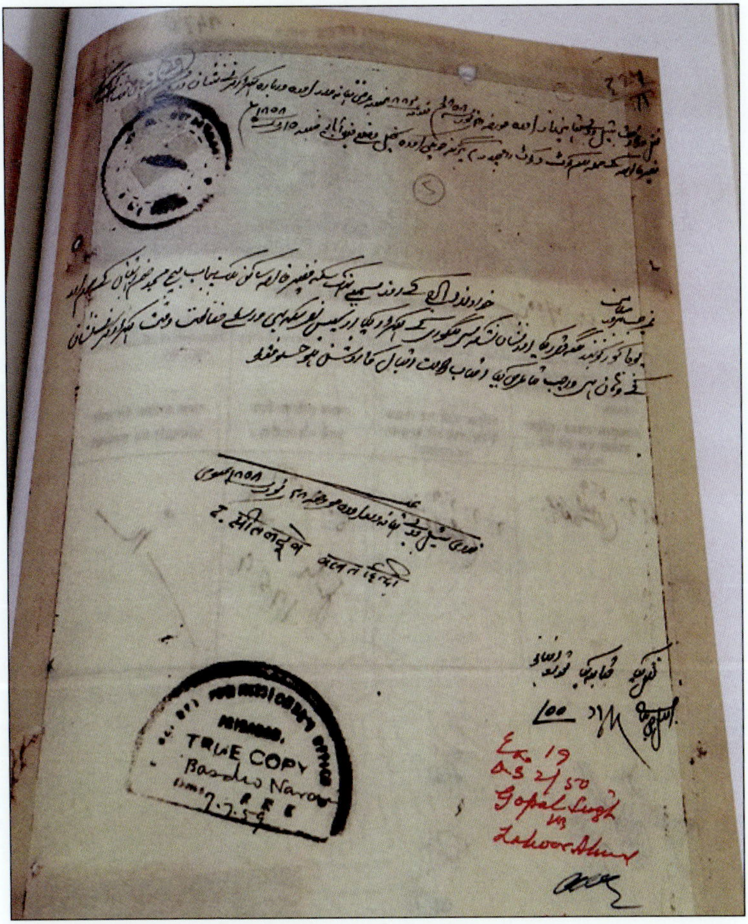

21. Report of the *thanedar* of Awadh dated 28th November 1858 on *havan* and *puja* inside Babri Masjid.

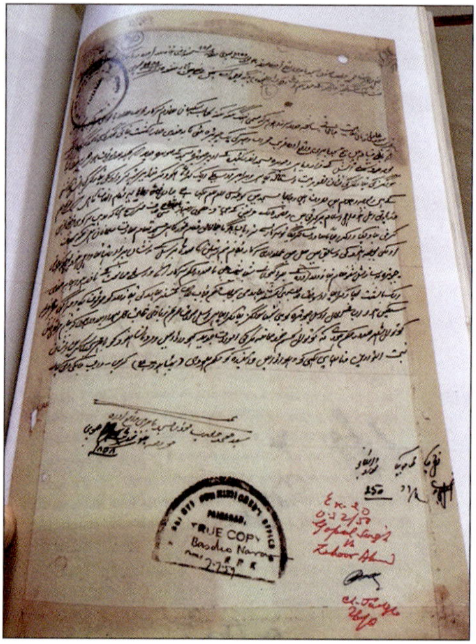

22. Muhammad Asghar's complaint of 30th November 1858 on *havan* and *puja* inside Babri Masjid.

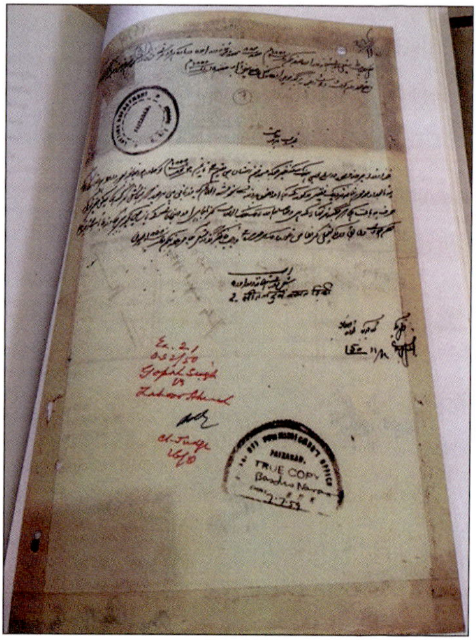

23. Report of the *thanedar* on eviction of Sikhs from Babri Masjid.

written, we confess we are deserving of whatever punishment the Government may decree.

In the second bond they affirmed,

> Whereas Gholam Husein and others, have given out that a Musjid existed in Hunooman Gurhee and on this, a disturbance arose between us, and the Mussulmans and as for the investigation of the matter three persons have been deputed – therefore, in the presence of those officers, and with our free will, we write, that if these three gentlemen will by examination and investigation prove that a musjid did exist in Hunooman Gurhee and will then issue their orders to us, we will readily agree thereto – on no account will we make any objections to what they may say – therefore, we have written this as a proof of what we have agreed to (Bhatnagar 1968: 123-24).

The Bairagis thereby committed to vacate Hanuman Garhi should any evidence be found that a masjid had existed inside the structure. They also produced *sanads* to prove that Nawabs Safdar Jang and Shuja-ud-daulah of Awadh had assisted them in the construction of certain buildings at Hanuman Garhi. The *sanads* made no reference to a masjid at Hanuman Garhi (Bhatnagar 1968: 125-27).

On 12th August 1855, Nawab Wajid Ali Shah sent a *purcha* to the British Resident, to which were attached five documents which established the long drawn out contest between Hindus and Muslims (N.A.I. Foreign Department Political, 28 December 1855, No. 351-358 & KW). The documents were:-

1. A document from Muhammad Nihalal-ud-din, the Darogah of Awadh, deputed by the King to ascertain whether any Masjid exists in Hanuman Garhi
2. A document from Hafeezullah, Darogah of Fyzabad
3. A document from the Imam of Fyzabad
4. A copy of a paper sealed with the seal of the Qazi of Fyzabad, dated AD 1735

5. A sealed statement by forty of the principal inhabitants of Fyzabad on the disturbances between Hindus and Muslims

The *purcha* stated a similar quarrel over the Masjid, built "by one of the former sovereigns of Delhi that this fact is notorious," had arisen in the time of Burhan-ul-Mulk Saadat Khan, the first Nawab of Awadh (1722-1739). But the Hindus had afterwards declared that they had no intention of "meddling with the mosque."

The Nawab asserted that "the tenor of all these papers cast (sic) all the blame on the Hindoos and details their atrocities." He further stated "A fence which was erected in the present king's reign to separate the Masjid from the Hindu place of worship has been torn down." In his reply of 14th August 1855, the Resident, commented that the enclosed representations were "obviously untrue in one particular," in as much as they laid the entire blame on the Hindus (N.A.I. Foreign Department Political, 28 Dec 1855; 351-58 & KW).

Meanwhile an Enquiry committee constituted to examine the case of a masjid at Hanuman Garhi unanimously decided in favour of the Bairagis. (Western descriptions of the temple three decades earlier had also not mentioned a mosque at the site; Cole 1988: 245).

The news of the decision of the Enquiry committee created a sensation among Muslims. Expressing the sentiments of his community, the Chief Minister told the British Resident that the Hindus had always been subjects of the Muslims;

> What matters if a dozen of their shrines were destroyed and their pollutions adorned with mosques? But the destruction of a mosque was an offence of the deepest hue; from all times it had been punished by mutilation, nay by death (N.A.I. Foreign Department Political, 28 December 1855, No. 450 & KW; Bhatnagar 1968: 137).

In September 1855, a new and more dangerous leader assumed charge of the struggle for Hanuman Garhi. A charismatic Sunni, Maulvi Amir Ali gave a call for *jihad* and gathered a number of working men and small shopkeepers, who gave up their businesses to follow him. The conflict took on wider proportions, Sunni against Shia, Muslim against Hindu. Wajid Ali Shah (a Shia) summoned Amir Ali to the palace for talks and proposed that a small mosque be attached to the temple. The suggestion was instantly rejected by the Bairagis (Cole 1988: 245-46; Llewellyn-Jones 2015: 110-12).

After all efforts at a settlement failed, British troops moved against Amir Ali and his followers before they could reach Ayodhya. Amir Ali was killed in an encounter lasting two hours (Bhatnagar 1968: 128-38).

Patrick Carnegy, the first British Commissioner and Settlement Officer in Faizabad, writing a decade and half later, described the conflict,

> The Janmasthan is within a few hundred paces of the Hanuman Garhi. In 1855, when a great rupture took place between the Hindus and Mohamedans, the former occupied the Hanuman Garhi by force, while the Musalmans took possession of the Janmasthan. The Mahomedans on that occasion actually charged up the steps of the Hanuman Garhi but were driven back with considerable loss. The Hindus then followed up this success, and at the third attempt, took the Janmasthan at the gate of which 75 Mahomedans are buried in the 'Martyrs' grave' (Ganjshahid). Several of the King's Regiment (the Awadh Nawab, Wajid Ali Shah) were looking on all the time, but their orders were not to interfere. It is said that up to that time the Hindus and Mahomedans alike used to worship in the mosque-temple. Since British rule a railing has been put up to prevent disputes, within which in the mosque the Mahomedans pray, while outside the fence the Hindus have raised a platform on which they make their offerings (Carnegy 1870: 20-21).

A.F. Mettell, in the *Report of the Settlement of the Land Revenue Fyzabad District,* also stated that till the conflict of 1855,

> ...the Hindus and Mahomedans alike used to worship in the mosque-temple. Since British rule, a railing has been put up to prevent disputes, within which in the mosque the Mahomedans pray, while outside the fence the Hindus have raised a platform on which they make their offerings (Mettell 1880: 236).

H.R. Nevill, too, recorded the open clash of 1855,

> ....the Musalmans occupying the Janamasthan in force and thence making a desperate assault on the Hanuman Garhi. They charged up the steps of the temple, but were driven back with considerable loss. The Hindus then made a counter-attack and stormed the Janamasthan, at the gate of which seventy-five Musalmans were buried, the spot being known as the Ganj Shahidan or the martyrs' resting place. Several of the King's regiments were present, but their orders were not to interfere. Shortly afterwards Maulvi Amir Ali of Amethi in Lucknow organized a regular expedition with the object of destroying the Hanuman Garhi; but he and his forces were stopped in the Bara Banki district. It is said that up to this time both Hindus and Musalmans used to worship in the same building, but since the mutiny an outer enclosure has been put up in front of the mosque and the Hindus, who are forbidden access to the inner yard, make their offerings on a platform which they have raised in the outer one (Nevill 1905: 179-80).

These reports expressly stated that till the clash of 1855, Hindus had free access to the inner precincts of the Masjid and openly offered prayers there.

LITIGATION AFTER 1857

The extensive evidence of court cases and proceedings after 1857 further highlighted the continuing Hindu claim to the site. It also reaffirmed that large crowds visited Ayodhya through the centuries, particularly on occasions like *Rama Navami*, and that special arrangements had to be made for pilgrims during these times.

A Report, dated 28th November 1858, by Sheetal Dubey, the *thanedar* of Oudh, is the first available record on the contest at the site. It referred to worship in the middle of Masjid Janam Asthan by a Nihang Singh Fakir Khalsa, a resident of Punjab. The Nihang had organized "*Havan* and *Puja* of Guru Govind Singh and erected a symbol of Sri Bhagwan, within the premises of the Masjid." The Report stated that twenty-five Sikhs had also been present for raising the religious flag at the Masjid Janam Asthan (pages 2298-99 para 2315).

PETITION OF MUHAMMAD ASGHAR (30.11.1858)

Two days later, Muhammad Asghar, the Khattib and Muezzin of Babri Masjid, made a representation to the British Government, on the matter. His complaint is the oldest individual and private document to throw light on the then prevailing situation. It stated that a Nihang Sikh, a resident of Punjab and a government employee, had constructed "an earth Chabutara" near the *Mihrab* and *Mimber*, and placed the picture of an idol,

> Fire has been lit there for light and *Puja* and *Home* is continuing there. In whole of this Masjid 'Ram Ram' has been written with coal.

Muhammad Asghar also declared that in the outer space of Babri Masjid (the courtyard within the walled boundaries of the mosque), Janamsthan had been lying desolate, where the Hindus had been worshipping for hundreds of years. He asserted that due to the conspiracy of *thanedar*, "the Bairagis constructed overnight a Chabutara up to height of one 'Balisht' until orders of injunction were issued." The Deputy Commissioner had suspended the *thanedar* and imposed a fine on the Bairagis. But "now the Chabootra has been raised to about 1¼ yards." Muhammad Asghar, therefore, requested that the Kotwal of the City visit the spot, get the new construction demolished, and the Hindus ousted; "the symbol and the idol may be removed from there and writing on the walls be washed ..." (pages 2300-03 para 2317).

As the authenticity of the document and the identity of the person who wrote it were unquestionable, the Allahabad High Court regarded it as irrefutable proof that Hindus prayed in the Masjid and the inner courtyard, as well as at the Ram Chabutara and Sita Rasoi in the outer courtyard (page 2304 para 2318). This would have been impossible had the entire premises been in Muslim possession (pages 2304-05 para 2319). Justice S.U. Khan noted that the Muslims had admitted that since the mid-nineteenth century the outer portion that contained the Ram Chabutara had been used by Hindus. Justice Khan also took cognizance of the fact that the dispute over the premises had been judicially noted in 1885, and in the records of various government officers since 1855 (Justice S.U. Khan page 5-6).

Despite several orders, it was only on 10th December 1858, that the *thanedar* reported that the "Jhanda (flag) was uprooted from the Masjid Janam Asthan and the Faqir residing therein was ousted" (pages 2309-10 para 2325). There was no mention of the performance of namaaz in Babri Masjid, or its revival, by Muslims (page 2310 para 2326).

Application of Mir Rajib Ali (5.11.1860)

The next record available is an application filed in the Court of the Deputy Commissioner, by Mir Rajib Ali, Khattib of Babri Masjid, requesting that the Chabutara which had been constructed inside Babri Masjid be removed. Mir Rajib Ali stated that a month ago, the Nihang respondent made a small Chabutara in the graveyard adjacent to Babri Masjid, which he was "extending day by day." Mir Rajib Ali also protested that,

> ...when the Moazzin recites Azaan, the opposite party begins to blow conch... (He wanted the) newly constructed Chabootra which had never existed, may kindly be demolished and a bond be got executed from the opposite party to the effect that he will not unlawfully and illegally interfere in the Masjid property and will not blow conch at the time of Azaan (pages 2313-17 para 2329).

On 12th March 1861, Mir Rajab Ali, Muhammad Asghar, and Muhammad Afzal reiterated their complaint of 5th November 1860. They stated that a Chabutara that had been built near Babri Masjid at Janam Asthan, had not been removed despite orders (page 2318 para 2331).

Complaint of Muhammad Afzal (25.9.1866)

Five years later, Muhammad Afzal, Mutawalli Babri Masjid, filed another complaint stating that about a month back the "Bairagiyan Janam Asthan Ram" had constructed a *kothri* "in an illegal manner within a few hours inside the compound of the mosque," with the intention of placing idols in it. Due to this construction, there had been "much rioting in the local populace." Muhammad Afzal wanted the *kothri* to be dismantled and the Masjid "protected from the fury of Bairagis." He affirmed,

> ... There had always been a tussle with Hindus who have ever been expressing their interests in the affairs of the Masjid...A good number of files of frequent such complaints in past are kept in the Collectorate. It was only due to the 'wisdom and justice of the Court,' that the Masjid could remain (page 2064 para 1978; pages 2341-46 para 2347).

Appeal of Muhammad Asghar (1877)

In the case of Mohammad Asghar Appellant vs. Mahant Baldeo Dass, an order was passed on 7th November 1873 for removal of the idol, i.e. *Charan Paduka*, said to have been created in the disputed building (page 2065 para 1979). Four years later, in

1877, Muhammad Asghar requested implementation of the order of 7th November 1873. He stated that as the *Charan Paduka* had not been removed, Mahant Baldeo Dass,

> ...has made a *Chulha* within the said compound which has never been done before. There was a small *Chulah* for *puja* which he has got extended ...each and every place within the boundary wall of the Mosque is that of the Mosque and its wall being the construction of Masjid itself ... should be entrusted to the Mutawalli of the Mosque and not to Hindu defendants. (The subordinate officer, however, had given permission to the defendants for) ... erecting a new door in the wall of the Masjid northwards. (This was a breach of the general principle because the defendants never had)... any concern with the wall of the Masjid ... The defendant belonging to other religion could not have been accorded permission to construct the door against religious canons... The respondent has cleverly done so for creating trouble in future. He wanted to spend more money to place idols along with the door (sic). It is a matter of justice that how idols could be placed on the wall of the Masjid which would be against all canons of Islam ...

Muhammad Asghar affirmed that there had been an "old controversy between the respondent and the appellant" and the Court had ordered that the respondent should not do anything new in that place. But, as Mahant Baldeo Dass Bairagi had gone underground, the order of 7th November 1873 could not be served on him. So the idol had not been removed as per Court orders..." (page 2065, para 1979; pages 2355-61 para 2352). The Allahabad High Court noted that the complaint was proof that in 1877, a *Chulha* also existed in the premises of Babri Masjid (page 2065 para 1980).

MOHAMMAD ASGHAR VS. KHEM DASS (1877)

The Deputy Commissioner of Faizabad submitted a report (not dated) pursuant to the order of the Faizabad Commissioner (dated 14th May 1877), passed in the appeal of

Mohammad Asghar. The Commissioner had asked for a report on a doorway in the wall dividing the mosque by a railing, which had been opened to provide a separate passage to visitors to the Janam Asthan on festival days. The Deputy Commissioner's report stated,

> A doorway has recently been opened in the wall of the Janam-Asthan not at all in Baber's mosque, but in the wall which in front is divided from the mosque by a railing. This opening was necessary to give a separate route on fair days to visitors to the Janam Asthan. There was one opening only, so the cruch (*sic*: rush) was very great and life was endangered. I marked out the spot for the opening myself so there is no need to depute any European officer. This petition is merely an attempt to annoy the Hindu by making it dependent on the pleasure of the mosque people to open or close the 2nd door in which the Mohammedans can have no interest (pages 2065-66 para 1981; pages 2361-63 para 2353).

The Commissioner dismissed the appeal, as the door in question had been opened by the Deputy Commissioner in the interest of public safety (page 2066 para 1982).

Justice S.U. Khan noted that initially there was just one door in the boundary wall towards the east. However, in 1877 another door was opened towards the north by the British authorities, which was "given under the control and management of Hindus in spite of severe objection by Muslims." The need for the second door arose because of the large number of Hindu devotees that gathered to worship at the Chabutara on two occasions a year, and in order to control the crowds. At what point in the northern wall the door should be opened was itself a subject of "raging dispute" between Hindus and Muslims. Ultimately a fragile truce was arrived at and it was agreed that the exact place should be marked by some European officer and that was accordingly done (Justice S.U. Khan pages 7-8).

Complaint by Mohammad Asghar (22.10.1882)

Mohammad Asghar filed a complaint against Raghubar Das, Mahant Janam Asthan, in October 1882, claiming rent for use of the Chabutara near the gate of the Masjid for the period 1288-1289 *Fasli* (AD 1881-1882). He stated,

> the courtyard and the Chabutara before the Masjid Janamsthan is the property of the plaintiff whereupon, from ancient times, is organized Mela Kartiki and Ram Navami. In other days shops of flowers and Batasha were being stalled, the contract wherefore was of Rs. 35/- per year. The plaintiff and the defendant had agreed to distribute this amount between themselves in the ratio of 50-50.

In 1288 *Fasli*, before *Kartik Asnan* and *Ram Navami*, the defendant, with *mala fide* intentions, made two shares of Rs. 30/- against the contract of Rs. 35/-, without the consent of the plaintiff, for both the festivals/fairs. Mohammad Asghar requested that a decree with costs be passed (pages 2371-75 para 2362).

The trial court dismissed the suit on 18th June 1883. Hari Kishan, Sub-Judge Faizabad, stated that Mohammad Asghar while claiming rent for the use of the Chabutara and Takht, had admitted that these were in possession of Raghubar Das, and had failed to uphold his claim for rent (page 2067, para 1985).

The Allahabad High Court noted that this application did not prove that continuous namaaz was being offered by the Muslim public. At *Rama Navami* and other fairs, some land was allowed to be used by outsiders for setting up shops. The Mutawalli shared the rental income with the priests of the Nirmohi Akhara, who managed the Chabutara and other religious structures in the outer courtyard (page 2423 para 2393).

Application of Mohammad Asghar (2.11.1883)

Mohammad Asghar filed another application as Mutawalli and Khattib of Babri Masjid, complaining that he was entitled to get the wall of the mosque white washed, but was being obstructed by Mahant Raghubar Das, who had the right only to the Chabutara and Sita ki Rasoi. He said the wall and the gate were part of the Mosque and he was at liberty to get them cleaned (pages 2067-69 para 1987). The Assistant Commissioner, Faizabad passed an order, on 22nd January 1884, whereby,

> ... Raghubar Das was restrained from carrying out repairs etc., in the internal and outer part of the compound and Mohammad Asghar was advised not to lock the outer door of the mosque ... The outer door will be left open. No lock will be allowed upon it. It is absolutely essential to observe the strictest neutrality and maintain the status quo (pages 2376-78 para 2365).

The Allahabad High Court observed that this order revealed intention of the authorities to thwart all hindrances to people visiting the disputed premises (pages 2066-67 para 1983; page 2376 para 2364).

Raghubar Das appealed to the Assistant Commissioner, on 27th June 1884, that despite the restraint, the Muslims "are doing whitewash at places where they never have done so. This fact will become clear from the inspection..." (pages 2378-80 para 2366).

Plaint by Mahant Raghubar Das (29.1.1885)

Sometime thereafter, Raghubar Das filed a suit, seeking permission to construct a temple over Chabutara Janam Asthan, measuring 21 feet by 17 feet, which was in his possession. He said that as there was no building over the Chabutara, he and others experienced great hardship "on account of excessive heat in summer and excessive cold and rain in rainy season." There could be no harm to anyone if a temple was constructed to cover the Chabutara; "if the temple is constructed the plaintiff and other faqirs and pilgrims will get facilities of every sort."

Raghubar Das stated that the Deputy Commissioner, Faizabad, had in 1883 prohibited construction of the temple due to objections raised by some Muslims. Thereupon he had petitioned the local self-Government, but on receiving no reply, gave notice to the office of the Secretary, Local Government. He got no response from there as well, which was why he had filed the present suit. The sole defendant was the Secretary of State for India in Council (page 1142 para 824; pages 2380-86 para 2367; Noorani I 2003: 175-76).

A map was attached with the complaint. The Sub-Judge, Faizabad, directed the Court's Commissioner, Gopal Sahai Amin, to prepare a map of the entire Babri Masjid premises. The map was almost identical to the one submitted by Raghubar Das. It showed that the inner courtyard and the constructed portion were with the Mohammedans and the outer courtyard including Sita ki Rasoi and Ram Chabutara in possession of the Hindus.

The Allahabad High Court observed that though it was uncertain when the Sita ki Rasoi was constructed, it was certainly before 1885. It stated,

> It is beyond comprehension that Mir Baqi or anyone else, while constructing a mosque at the disputed place could have spared some Hindu structure (s) to continue, ... in the precincts of the mosque so as to be worshipped by Hindus inside the premises of mosque. We put this question to Sri Jilani also and he frankly stated that no Muslim would allow idol worship in the precinct of a mosque (page 2069 para 1989).

The Court was, therefore, of the view that when the Masjid was first constructed no Hindu structure could have been permitted to exist in the premises. But, the Masjid appeared to have been deserted soon after its construction. The local Hindus availed of the opportunity to raise a symbolic structure to continue worship at the site they believed to be the birthplace of Rama. That was how the *vedi* existed in the courtyard of the Masjid, and was noticed by Tieffenthaler (page 1767 para 1642; page 1768 para 1644).

Statement of Mohammad Asghar

In response to Mahant Raghubar Das's suit seeking permission to construct a temple over the Rama Chabutara, Mohammad Asghar filed a written statement on 22nd December 1885 (pages 1143-44 para 827; page 1146 para 832). Therein he stated that Babur had constructed the mosque and got the word "Allah" engraved on its door and granted *Maafi* for its expenses. No one else could claim the right of construction there. Until the king, or any of his successors, gave permission or gave any part of the land, the plaintiff, Mahant Raghubar Das, could not become owner of the land. Raghubar Das had not submitted any documentary evidence regarding the ownership of the Chabutara; therefore he had no right to build a *mandir* over it. Mohammad Asghar asserted,

> ... for 368 years generally and from 1857, in particular, the plaintiff could not produce any document to show his ownership. He can never have any right to construct any temple on the floor of the Masjid. The claim of the plaintiff that the Chabutara is theirs and thereby acquired right to construct any temple, is a mere misunderstanding because the plaintiff has no ownership right or liberty to use the Chabutara or offer gift (*charhawa*) over the chabutara... (pages 2387-95 para 2370).

Justice S.U. Khan noted that Mohammad Asghar did not deny the correctness of the map presented by Raghubar Das (Justice S.U. Khan page 17).

The report of the Amin Commission on this case, dated 6th December 1885 was of considerable importance. It showed that Sita Rasoi, Chabutra, Janmasthan, and Chappar (enclosurement) of the disciple (Chela) of the Mahant were all situated within the boundary wall of the site where the Masjid stood. Beyond the boundary wall and just adjacent to it was a deep depression pathway on all the four sides (*parikarma*) of the pilgrims (*khai parikarma har chahar taraf*). In other words, the entire area site enclosed by the *parikarma* was the sacred Janmasthan (Grover 2015: 288).

The case was heard by Pandit Hari Kishan, Sub Judge Faizabad. After visiting the site, in his judgement on 24th December 1885, he observed,

> ...on seeing the spot it is evident that *charan* (i.e. feet) is embossed on the Chabutara which is being worshipped. On a Chabutara over that Chabutara an idol of Thakurji is installed. The Chabutara is in possession of the plaintiff and whatever offering made, is taken away by the plaintiff and this fact also admitted to Mohammad Asghar defendant. The witnesses of the plaintiff also prove the possession of the plaintiff for this reason that there is a pucca wall like a fence constructed to fix the boundaries of land held by Muslims and Hindus ... The witnesses for the defendant plead their ignorance of the possession of the plaintiff over the Chabutara. In between the mosque and the Chabutara is a wall which can be fully evident from the perusal of the corrected plan prepared by the Amin and it is clear that there are separate boundaries between the mosque and the Chabutara and this fact is also supported by the fact that there is a boundary wall built by the Government before the recent dispute. Before this Hindus and Muslims both used to offer prayer and worship at that place. In 1855, after the fight amongst Hindus and Muslims, a boundary wall was constructed to avoid future disputes, so that the Muslims should worship inside that wall and the Hindus should worship outside that wall, hence the Chabutara and the land which is situated outside the boundary wall belong to Hindus and the plaintiff.

The Sub Judge, however, pointed that that this place was not like other places where the owner had the right to construct any building he liked. For,

> The prayer for permission to construct the temple is at such a place where there is only one passage for the temple as well as for the mosque. The place where the Hindus worship is in their possession from of old and their ownership cannot be questioned and around it there is the wall of the mosque and the word Allah is inscribed on it. If a temple is constructed on the Chabutara at such a place then there will be sound of bells of the temple and *shankh* when both Hindus and Muslims pass from the same way, and if permission is given to Hindus for constructing temple then one day or the other a criminal case will be started and thousands of people will be killed (Noorani I 2003: 178-81).

The pro-temple group pointed out in the Allahabad High Court that it was significant that Mohammad Asghar did not then state that the Janmasthan Temple at Ram's birthplace already existed separately at a distance of 60-70 steps from the Disputed Structure, as was now being claimed by Left historians (page 4449-50 para 4092).

Mahant Raghubar Das's case was also heard by the District Judge, Faizabad, Col. F.E.A. Chamier. After a visit to the site, he stated in his judgement of 18/26 March 1886,

> It is most unfortunate that a masjid should have been built on land specially held sacred by the Hindus, but as that event occurred 356 years ago it is too late now to remedy the grievance. All that can be done is to maintain the parties in status quo. In such a case as the present one any umonation could cause more harm and derangement of order than benefit. The entrance to the enclosure is under a gateway which bears the superscription 'Allah' — immediately on the left is the platform or chabutara of masonry occupied by the Hindus. On this is a small superstructure of wood in the form of a tent ...

Chamier dismissed the suit as there was "no *'injuria,'* nothing which would give a right of action to the plaintiff (Noorani I 2003: 182-84).

The Officiating Judicial Commissioner, W. Young, delivered his judgement in the case on 1st November 1886. He noted that the Hindus of Ayodhya wanted to create a new temple over the Chabutara. This spot was situated within the precinct of the grounds surrounding a mosque erected some 350 years ago, "owing to the bigotry and tyranny of the Emperor Babur, who purposely chose this holy spot according to Hindu legend as the site of his mosque." He also observed that the Hindus seem to have got very limited rights of access to certain spots within the precincts adjoining the mosque and "they have for a series of years been persistently trying to increase those rights and to erect buildings on two spots in the enclosure." These were the Sita ki Rasoi and Ram Chandar ki Janam Bhumi. He too was against any change in the status quo (Noorani I 2003: 186-88).

Riots in Ayodhya - 1912

On 20th and 21st November 1912, riots broke out in Ayodhya and Fyzabad on the issue of cow sacrifice on the occasion of Bakr-Id. A letter from R. Burn, Chief Secretary in the Government of the United Provinces, to the Secretary to the Government of India, Home Department, dated 25th January 1913, stated,

> One perpetual cause of friction was the existence of a mosque on the traditional site of Ram's birthplace. This was constructed in 1528 by the Emperor Babar who destroyed the ancient temple and used its materials for the new building.

The letter said that before the annexation of Oudh in 1856 there had been many occasions on which bitterness between Hindus and Muhammadans resulted in bloodshed. After the

Mutiny, however, there had been no major trouble till the recent events. This was due to the fact that the Muhammadan residents of Ajodhya were now "of comparatively little importance and have not been in a position to assert themselves against the powerful associations occupying the numerous Hindu temples and religious establishments." In 1911, of a total population of 12,575, Hindus numbered 10,927 and Muhammadans 1,623 (N.A.I. Home Political Branch B April 1913, Nos. 109-114: 39-43).

The Lieutenant-Governor visited Fyzabad on 18th July 1915 to find a solution acceptable to Hindus and Muslims on the issue of cow-slaughter in Ayodhya. He observed,

> It is very difficult ...for anyone who is not a Hindu to appreciate the reverence which they feel for the holy ground of Ayodhya... (N.A.I. Home Political Branch A, October 1915, Nos. 258-259: 5-6).

THE RIOTS OF 1934

Riots broke out again in Ayodhya, on 27th March 1934, at the time of Bakr-Id. The Commissioner of Fyzabad provided details of the outbreak to the Chief Secretary of the United Provinces, the following day. He stated that the immediate provocation was the performance of cow sacrifice in nearby Shahjahanpur, where there was no official record of cow sacrifice earlier, though there had been hints of unrest at Bakr-Id in 1932. Meanwhile, in Ayodhya, a large crowd of Bairagis attacked Babri Masjid, which was located "in a more or less isolated position well away from the main road." It was some time before the Deputy Collector heard of it. He went with five policemen, all the force he had with him. He found at least 200 Bairagis "at work demolishing the mosque ..." (N.A.I. Home Department – Political F. No. 5/2/1934 Poll: 4-6). The Deputy Collector reported,

> The Bairagis have done very considerable damage to the mosque. The gateway has been demolished almost entirely. Fitments inside have been burnt. The metal pinnacles on the tops (sic) of the three main domes have been removed, and on at least one of the domes substantial damage has been done to the masonry, also to subsidiary masonry work elsewhere (N.A.I. Home Department – Political F. No. 5/2/1934 Poll: 6).

On 16th April 1934, H. Bomford, Chief Secretary to the Government of the United Provinces, informed M.G. Hallett, Chief Secretary to the Government, Home Department, that orders had been issued that a punitive police force would be imposed at the expense of the Hindu inhabitants of Ayodhya and orders also given to assess the damage "in order to facilitate disposal of claims." The information that the damage would be paid for had "given general satisfaction to Muslim visitors there" (N.A.I. Home Department – Political F. No. 5/2/1934 Poll: 19-20). The fine of Rs. 85,000 as compensation to Muslims aroused considerable resentment among Hindus and many representations were made to the Government (N.A.I. Home Department – Political F. No. 5/2/1934 Poll: 42-45, 56-58).

Letter of Kalab Husain, Mutawalli of Babri Masjid (20.11.1943)

Thereafter information on the state of affairs at Babri Masjid came from a letter to the Secretary, Sunni Waqf Board, Lucknow, by Kalab Husain, Mutawalli of Babri Masjid. It stated that the floor mats used for sitting at the time of namaaz were "available only to the extent of routine use." The remaining floor mats were kept separately with Maulvi Abdul Gaffar, Pesh Imam. They were brought by the Muezzin on Fridays and returned to the same place after namaaz, as most of the mattresses had been stolen from the mosque. The letter added that "this mosque has been built on such a place where often riots took place and every year there is apprehension of breach of peace" (pages 2940-47 para 3103).

The Allahabad High Court observed that this was an admission that only Friday prayers were offered at Babri Masjid and the outer courtyard was out of Muslim control (page 2947).

Report of Muhammad Ibrahim, Inspector of Waqf (10.12.1948)

The Inspector of Waqf, Muhammad Ibrahim, filed a report in regard to Babri Masjid which confirmed continuing tensions at the site. It stated,

> On investigation in Faizabad city it was revealed that because of the fear of Hindus and Sikhs no one goes into the Masjid to pray Namaz Isha. If by chance any passenger stays in the Masjid he is being put in trouble by the Hindus. Out of the Sahan of Masjid there is a temple where many Pandas reside and they harass the Muslims whosoever visit inside the mosque. I went at the spot and from inquiries it was revealed that the said allegations are correct. Locals went on saying to the extent that there is great danger to mosque from Hindus that they may harm its walls etc (pages 2950-52; Noorani I 2003: 203-04).

Second report of Muhammad Ibrahim (23.12.1948)

A fortnight later, Muhammad Ibrahim presented another report, wherein he described his visit to Ayodhya the previous day. He mentioned that Baba Sukhdas had visited Ayodhya three months earlier and while addressing the Bairagis and *pujaris* said that *Ramayana patha* should be recited at the birthplace. The news had spread to the surrounding areas and within a month hundreds of *pujaris* and *pandits* had assembled there. The recitation of the *Ramayana patha* had been going on for weeks, during which time the area in front of the Masjid was dug up by the Bairagis and a flag hoisted there.

Several graves were also exhumed. Muhammad Ibrahim reported,

> There is always a lock on the Masjid. There is no namaz or *ajan* at any time. The keys of the lock of the Masjid are with the Muslims. Police do not allow the lock to be opened. On Fridays for about two to three hours ... the cleaning and sweeping is done and *Shube* namaz is also done. Then it is locked. At the time of the *Shube* namaz, a lot of noise is created, and when the *namazis* leave, from the surrounding houses shoes and stones are hurled towards the *namazis*. ... Mr. Lohia also visited Ayodhya ... The bairagees said the Masjid is Janmabhumi, and so give it to us. ... I spent the night in Ayodhya, and the bairagees are forcibly taking possession of the Masjid. Today it is Jumma, I visited the site, and what do I see there: ten or fifteen bairagees armed with *lathis* and *farsa*, and many others with sticks in their hands are standing near the gate of the Masjid. Many are also collecting there from nearby... (pages 2952-57; Noorani I 2003: 204-05).

The Allahabad High Court observed that the report established that Hindus continued to enter the inner courtyard and worship there. No restrictions were imposed on their entry. Further, at least three non-Muslim structures existed in outer courtyard, where also worship went on unhindered (page 1979 para 1903).

Initial Attempts to Construct a Rama temple

After independence, the Hindu public presented an application to the UP Government on the construction of a Rama temple near the mosque.[2] In his report of 10th October 1949, the City Magistrate stated,

> Hindu public has put in this application with a view to erect a decent and *vishal* temple instead of the small one which exists at present. There is nothing in the way and permission can be given as Hindu population is very keen

to have a nice temple at the place where Bhagwan Ram Chandra Ji was born. The land where temple is to be erected is of Nazul (Noorani I 2003: 205-07).

Installation of the Image

On 23rd December 1949, a First Information Report (FIR) was filed by the Senior Sub-Inspector in charge *Thana* Ayodhya, that a group of 50 to 60 persons had entered the Babri Masjid the previous night and placed an idol of Sri Rama in the mosque. Significantly, no Muslim came forward to lodge an FIR, or complain of dispossession, or obstruction, in his alleged use of the Masjid.

In a letter to the Chief Secretary, Bhagwan Sahai, dated 26th December 1949, the Deputy Commissioner/ D.M. Faizabad, K.K.K. Nayar pointed to "the immense public sympathy in support of this cause." In another letter to the Chief Secretary, on 27th December 1949, Nayar said that the Commissioner had given him and the Superintendent of Police a scheme for surreptitiously removing the idol from the mosque. He described the idea of the removal of the idol as "fraught with the gravest danger to public peace over the entire district and must lead to a conflagration, of horror unprecedented in the annals of this controversy." The Hindus, with no exception, were for keeping the idol in situ, and "are ready to kill and die in this cause. The depth of feeling behind the movement and the desperate nature of the resolves and vows in support of it should not be underestimated..." He added, "I shall also be unable to find in the district a Hindu, let alone a qualified priest, who will be prepared on any inducement to undertake the removal of the idol."

Nayar offered a solution for the Government's consideration. He suggested that the mosque be attached and both Hindus and Muslims be excluded from it, with the exception of a few *pujaris* who would offer *bhog* and *puja* before the idol, which could continue. The parties would be referred to the Civil Court for adjudication of rights. No attempt would be made to hand over possession to the Muslims till the Civil Court, if at all, decreed the claim in their favour (Noorani I 2003: 210-18). Nayar's suggestion was supported by the Divisional Commissioner, who proposed keeping the site under police control and allowing a priest to perform the requisite worship till excitement had lessened and a plan could be worked out with leaders of the Hindu and Muslim communities.

Thereafter, on 29th December 1949, Markanday Singh, the Additional City Magistrate, Faizabad-cum-Ayodhya, ordered attachment of the property under Section 145 Criminal Procedure Code 1898 and appointed Priya Dutt Ram, Chairman, Municipal Board, as receiver to take care of the property. The receiver took charge on 5th January 1950 and immediately took steps to ensure continuance of *bhog* and *puja* (*Muslim India* 53, May 1987). And *puja* at the site has continued uninterrupted since then.

END NOTES

1. Wajid Ali Shah was known for his fascination for Lord Krishna, and directed a play on the Lord's deeds. In 1853, 1854, and 1855, he also held *Sawan Melas,* when the courtyard of Qaisarbagh Palace was thrown open to the public (Llewellyn-Jones 2015: 54-55)

   However, there had been trouble within a month of his coronation. One of the city's news-writers sent a report on an apparently appalling event. A jeweller, named Chhote Lal, was alleged to have slit the throat of a young Brahmin boy and sacrificed him to "the Idol Purasnath" (Parsunath) in a newly constructed temple (NAI: Foreign Political Consultations, 24 March 1847, No. 94).

   Without pausing to reflect on the news, Wajid Ali Shah dispatched men to demolish the temple. Around fifty jewellers marched to the palace to protest the false report and demolition, but were turned away by palace guards.

The next day, the Nawab again sent his workmen and three more temples were destroyed. Taking advantage of the disturbance, one of the king's companion-servants, Mir Mahdi, sent a hired ruffian to Haiderganj, where several Shiva temples were destroyed.

The superintendent of police, Ali Riza Khan, then sent a communication stating that no killing of a Brahmin boy had taken place, and that the jeweller caste of Hindus (most likely Jains) would not kill an insect, much less shed human blood. But by then the damage had been done (Llewellyn-Jones 2015: 68-70).

2. It is interesting to note that in March 1783, a Sikh chieftain Baghel Singh set up his camp in Delhi and began to reclaim sites connected with the Gurus in the city. At the site of the execution of Guru Tegh Bahadur was constructed the Sis Ganj Gurudwara, at the site of his cremation the Rakab Ganj Gurudwara, at the site of the residence of Guru Har Krishen, Bangla Sahib Gurudwara, and at the site where the infant Guru and the wife of Guru Gobind Singh were cremated, Bala Sahib Gurudwara (Khushwant Singh I 2015: 170).

7

Left Historians Intervene

Left historians joined the Ayodhya debate in November 1989, when the Centre for Historical Studies, Jawaharlal Nehru University (JNU), issued *"The Political Abuse of History: Babri Masjid-Ramjanmabhumi Dispute – An Analysis by Twenty-five Historians."* Professors S. Gopal, Romila Thapar, and Bipin Chandra headed the list of signatories.

The historians argued that Ayodhya's rise as a major centre of Rama worship was, "relatively recent." Well before that, the city was sacred to the Buddhists and Jains. The cult of Rama, they stated, acquired popularity only from the thirteenth century, and gained ground with the steady rise of the Ramanandi sect and the composition of Rama's story in Hindi. But even in the fifteenth and sixteenth centuries, Shaivism was more important than the cult of Rama. Ramanandi *sadhus* began to settle in large numbers in Ayodhya only from the eighteenth century. Later, they built most of their temples in the city. According to the JNU historians there was no mention of the demolition of a Ramjanmabhumi temple at Ayodhya before the nineteenth century. Neither Abul Fazl nor Tulsidas referred to it. The JNU historians also questioned the assumption that "Muslim rulers were invariably and naturally opposed to the sacred places of Hindus." They recommended that the Ramjanmabhumi/Babri Masjid be declared "a national monument."

Some months later, on 10th February 1990, Professor R.S. Sharma delivered the Mamidipudi Venkatarangaiyya Memorial Lecture on "Communalism and India's Past," at the XIV session of the Andhra Pradesh History Congress. This was published as a small monograph titled, *Communal History and Rama's Ayodhya*. Professor Sharma rejected the view that Islam almost extinguished Hindu culture or that Hindus in medieval times perceived the invaders from Central Asia in "purely religious or Islamic terms." He blamed colonial historians and archaeologists for setting "the communal trap," in which "some important Indian historians" got caught (Sharma 1990: 8-11).

Professor Sharma reiterated the arguments of the JNU historians on Ayodhya. He said that Ayodhya "has not been a *tirtha* of a very long standing." It emerged as a place of religious pilgrimage only in medieval times. Kanaka Bhavan, the earliest Rama temple in Uttar Pradesh, dated to the seventeenth century (Sharma 1990: 24-27). Professor Sharma was categorical that there was "not a shred of historical evidence" to support the view that a Rama temple was built in Ayodhya in the eleventh-twelfth centuries. There was "nothing to show that a Rama temple was demolished and a mosque raised in its place." Professor Sharma lamented that "a lover of Hindu art and architecture (Babar) should be credited with the destruction of a Rama temple, which, in any case, did not exist." He, too, wanted Babri Masjid to be treated "as a national monument" (Sharma 1990: 26-30).

Professor Romila Thapar, in her turn, was critical of the alleged elevation of Valmiki's *Ramayana* in the ongoing dispute. In April 1990, speaking on "Different Versions of the

Ramayana," in Delhi, she censured the projection of Valmiki's *Ramayana* and Tulsidas's *Ramacharitamanas* as the sole authentic rendition of Rama's story (*The Telegraph* 19 April 1990). Professor Thapar repeated this argument on numerous occasions, stating that what was of the "greatest interest" about the Rama *katha* was "its multiple versions." The purpose of each version was significant, and they could not "all be labelled as manifestations of a single religious expression" (Thapar 1989, 1991, 2005: 333-59).

VALMIKI *RAMAYANA* – THE FUNDAMENTAL TEXT

Contrary to Left assertions, Valmiki's narrative is widely acknowledged as the earliest surviving account of Rama's life. The religious significance of Rama evolved on the basis of his depiction in Valmiki's work. It was around the core of Valmiki's story that subsequently developed the view of Rama as God incarnate. The numerous retellings of the *Ramayana* (three hundred according to Camille Bulke) were retellings of Valmiki's story that everyone was familiar with. No other version ever matched the repute of Valmiki's *Ramayana* (Pollock 1993: 263).

Rama's story occurred in three early Buddhist texts — the *Dasharatha Kathanam*, the *Anamakam Jatakam*, and the *Dasharatha Jataka*. The first of these, *Dasharatha Kathanam*, belonged to the first-second century AD. The original text is no longer available. A Chinese translation of AD 472 survives. The *Anamakam Jatakam* gave an altered version of the *Ramayana*, but mentioned no character by name. The *Dasharatha Jataka* (Cowell IV 1901: No. 461) presented a tale narrated by Gautama Buddha in Jetavana, on observing the sorrow of a land-owner whose father had died. Buddha said to the man, "Lay Brother, wise men of old who exactly knew the eight conditions of the world, felt at a father's death no grief ..." and began to relate the story of Rama. Concluding the story Buddha said,

> At that time the king Suddhodana [Buddha's father] was the king Dasaratha, Mahamayi [Buddha's mother] was the mother, Rahula's mother was Sita, Ananda was Bharat, and I myself was Rama-pandita.

Most scholars have not regarded the *Dasharatha Jataka* older than the Valmiki *Ramayana,* and view it as "merely a distortion of the same" (Kane Vol. I Part I 1990: 392; Gombrich 1985: 427-37). Left historian Suvira Jaiswal, however, denied the centrality of Valmiki's *Ramayana;* and described the *Dasaratha Jataka* as "the earliest documentation of the Rama legend..." (Jaiswal 2013: 123).

Among the oldest Jain versions of Rama's legend was the *Vasudevahindi* of Sanghadasa (third or fourth century AD), in Prakrit. Another early Jain work, also in Prakrit, was the *Paumachariya* of Vimala Suri, dated between the third and sixth century AD (Shah 1983: 58; 62-63). The third major Jain text, the *Uttarapurana* by Gunabhadra, was composed in Sanskrit (Brockington 1984: 266). The Jain versions were all much later than Valmiki's, and were "unmistakably" indebted to him (Kulkarni 1980: 241).

WAS AYODHYA A BUDDHIST AND JAIN CITY?

Ayodhya was sacred to the Buddhists and Jains. Buddha himself was believed to have preached in the city. The Chinese travellers, Fa-Hien and Huien Tsang, attested to the existence of over a hundred Buddhist monasteries in Ayodhya (Law 1976: 67-69). The first and fourth Jain *Tirthankaras* were born in the city. Like Rama, Buddha and the Jain *Tirthankaras* were scions of the Ikshvakus. Over time Buddhist and Jain influence declined, while Rama worship remains a living tradition.

IDENTIFICATION OF AYODHYA

Left historians have questioned the identification of present day Ayodhya with the Ayodhya of ancient times, which they have located in Afghanistan and even Egypt. Indian tradition, however, never demonstrated any uncertainty on this count.

Ayodhya figured significantly in early Jain literature. In the *Vasudevahindi* (third or fourth century AD), Sanghadasa stated, "In the north or Sravasti janapada, not far, is located the Kosala janapada, which is prominent among all *janapadas*. There is situated Saketa, the best of the cities. In that city there is an extremely beautiful village known as Ramaniya..." Sanghadasa said that as the residents of the city were modest, Indra commanded his attendant to name it Vinita (Jain 1994: 90-91). In Jain works Ayodhya was designated as Aujjha, Kosala, Ikkhagabhumi, and Ramapuri (Jain 1994: 90-91; Aggarwal and Chowdhry 1991: 4-5).

Buddha's stay in Ayodhya was associated and commemorated with this very city. Also, in popular memory, none but the present city was accepted as Rama's Ayodhya. Kalidasa, in his *Raghuvamsha,* mentioned Saketa several times. The commentator, Mallinatha, explained these verses - 'Of Saketa' i.e. of Ayodhya (Agrawal 1994: 61).

Interestingly, Professor R.S. Sharma's former student, Suvira Jaiswal, deposed in the Allahabad High Court,

> It is also true that the present Ayodhya is the same old Ayodhya... It is also true that it is found from the sources of Jain religion that Saket and Ayodhya are the same. ... It is also true to say that at many places, Lord Rama has been referred to as Koshal Naresh (King of Koshal) (pages 4935-36 para 4378).

AYODHYA: A *TIRTHA*

According to Left historians Tulsidas attached no importance to Ayodhya as the birthplace of Rama. Tulsi, however, came from Banaras to commence his work in the birthplace and on the birthday of Rama. In his opening verses he wrote,

> Placing my head on the feet of Sri Hari I commence this story in the Samvat year 1631 (AD 1574). On Tuesday, the ninth of the lunar month of Caitra, this story shed its lustre at Ayodhya. On this day of Sri Rama's birth the presiding spirits of all holy places flock there — so declare the Vedas — and demons, Nagas, birds, human beings, sages and gods come and pay their homage to the Lord of Raghus. Wise men celebrate the great birthday festival and sing the sweet glory of Sri Rama. Numerous groups of pious men take dip in the holy water of the Sarayu and, visualizing in their heart the beautiful swarthy form of Sri Rama mutter His name.

Rama while showing his city to the *vanaras*, Sugriva, Angada, and Vibhishana said,

> ... Although all have extolled Vaikuntha (my divine Abode), which is familiar to the Vedas and the Puranas and known throughout the world, it is not so dear to Me as the city of Ayodhya: only some rare soul knows this secret. This beautiful city is My birthplace; to the north of it flows the holy Saryu, by bathing in which men secure a home near Me without any difficulty. The dwellers here are very dear to me; the city is not only full of bliss itself but bestows a residence in My divine Abode.

The *vanaras* were all delighted to hear these words of the Lord and said, "Blessed indeed is Ayodhya, that has evoked praise from Sri Rama Himself!" (pages 4758-9 para 4304; *Sri Ramacharitamanasa, Balakanda - Chaupai* 1-4, *doha* 34, page 33 and *Uttarakanda chaupai* 1-4 page 679; Gita Press, 1st edition 1968, 11th edition 1999).

EVOLUTION OF RAMA CULT

The literary, sculptural, and epigraphic evidence clearly indicates that by the fourth-fifth century AD, the Rama cult had been established and had all-India prevalence. By then the evolution of Rama from epic hero to incarnation of Vishnu to Supreme Reality had been more or less completed (Jacobi 1960: 50-51; Brockington 1984: 324-26; Desai 1973: 115-16; Bhandarkar 1913: 47, 65-66).

In the fourth-fifth century AD, Kalidasa, court-poet of the imperial Guptas and ranked next only to Valmiki as a great *Ramayana* poet, stressed the divinity of Rama. In his *Raghuvamsha,* he described Rama as *Ramabhidhano Hari,* Hari known as Rama (Raychaudhuri 1920: 174). Prabhavatigupta, the Vakataka queen and daughter of the Gupta emperor, Chandragupta II, was also a Rama devotee. The two inscriptions she issued in the last quarter of the fourth century AD suggest that a sanctuary dedicated to Rama was situated on top of Ramagiri hill (modern Ramtek), probably enshrining his (*pada*) footprints *(Corpus Inscriptionum Indicarum* Vol. V 1963: 5-9, *33-37;* Mirashi Vol. IV 1966: 48).

Kalidasa, who visited the Vakataka kingdom at the behest of his Gupta monarch, mentioned Ramagiri in his *Meghaduta.* Prabhavati's son, Pravarasena II, is credited with the authorship of *Setubandha,* in which Rama was regarded identical with Vishnu and not simply his incarnation. Pravarasena II built a temple dedicated to Rama in his new capital, Pravarapura (probably modern Paunar, Wardha), where he shifted sometime between AD 431 and 439 (*Corpus Inscriptionum Indicarum* Vol. V 1963: xli).

Sculpted panels found at Paunar, dating to the mid-fifth century, are among the oldest pieces of archaeological evidence testifying to the iconographic representation of Rama (*Corpus Inscriptionum Indicarum* Vol. V 1963: lx-lxii). Slightly later are the *Ramayana* panels at the temple at Deogarh, Jhansi (*Memoirs* 70 ASI 1999). The depiction of the story in stone occurred alongside its popularity in contemporary literature.

Apart from the *Ramopakhyana* (the *Mahabharata* version of the Rama story) and presentations in older *Puranas,* like the *Vishnu* and *Brahmanda Puranas,* and Bhasa's *Pratima* and *Abhisheka Natakas;* Rama's story was the subject of several works

24. A 2nd-1st century BCE terracotta from Kaushambi showing Ravana carrying away Sita.

25. A terracotta figure from Nachara Khera, with the name Rama inscribed in Brahmi characters of the 3rd century CE.

26. Terracotta from Bhitargaon showing a scene from the *Ramayana*, 5th century CE, presently in Brooklyn Museum, U.S.A.

27. Ahalya offering fruits to Rama, 5th century CE, Deogarh, presently in National Museum, Delhi.

28. Ramayana scenes from the Durga temple, Aihole, Karnataka.

30. *Vanaras*, Hoysalesvara temple, Halebid.

31. Sri Rama giving *abhignam* (ring) to Hanuman, Halebid.

29. Rama, Vali, and Sugriva from the Papanatha temple, Karnataka.

32. A depiction of Rama from the Pattabhirama temple, Hampi.

33. The Hazare Rama temple, Hampi.

34. Rama and Lakshman as depicted at the Gandha Madhana hill, Hampi.

35. Akbar's Rama Siya coins.

36. Rama and Lakshmana bemoaning the loss of Sita, Pahari School, Kangra, 1780-1785.

in Sanskrit and Prakrit. In addition to Kalidasa's *Raghuvamsha* and Pravarasena's *Setubandha,* may be mentioned the Prakrit text, *Vasudevahindi,* of Sanghadasa; *Paumachariya* of the Jain teacher, Vimala Suri (fourth century AD); and Bhatti's *Ravanavadha* (probably sixth century AD).

Professor John Brockington expressed the view that "too little weight" had been given to the literary, sculptural, and epigraphic evidence. While it may not suffice to suggest that Rama was universally seen as an *avatara* of Vishnu in the fifth century AD, it did imply "a special status for him" (Brockington 1998: 472).

EARLY EVIDENCE OF *RAMAYANA*

Kautilya (fourth century BC) was familiar with the central themes of the *Ramayana* and *Mahabharata.* In the *Arthashastra,* he advised that no one should emulate Ravana or Duryodhana for that was the path of ruin;

"*manadravanah paradaranaprayachchhan; Duryodhano rajyadamsam cha*" – Ravana perished because he was unwilling to restore a stranger's wife, and Duryodhana, because he was averse to part with a portion of his kingdom *Arthashastra* (1.6. 8).

The *Mahavibhasha* composed possibly during the reign of the Kushan ruler, Kanishka (second century AD), contained the earliest mention of the word *Ramayana* and its size. It stated that the book called *Ramayana* had 12,000 *shlokas* and focused on two themes, Sita's abduction by Ravana and her rescue by Rama.

In the second century AD, the Buddhist writer, Kumaralata, in his *Kalpanamanditika* mentioned public recitation of the *Ramayana.* In the sixth century AD, Varahamihira, in his *Brhatsamhita,* formulated rules for making images of Rama.

In the thirteenth century, Hemadri Pandit, the renowned minister of Ramachandra, the Yadava king of Devagiri, prepared a *dharmanibandha,* or "law code," with liturgical instructions for worshipping Rama as an incarnation, and described the *raghavadvadasivrata,* a ceremony connected with his birth. Hemadri also reproduced a part of the *Agastya Samhita,* a twelfth century work, which was possibly the first to deal with the important festival of *Rama Navami.*

In the fourteenth century, the ascetic, Ramananda, laid strong foundations for the devotional worship of Rama. The Ramanandi sect he founded performed a particularly significant role in the development of Hindu religion and Hindi literature. Before Tulsidas's *Ramacharitamanas,* Ramananda's *Ramarakshastrotra* was the major work in Hindi on Rama.

The first reference to the staging of Rama plays occurred in the *Harivamsha.* Jinapalopadhyaya, a Jain writer of the early thirteenth century, also referred to Rama plays. Tulsidas's *Ramacharitamanas* (written in AD 1574) was enacted during *Ramlila* celebrations in several parts of the country, particularly Banaras.

THE *RAMAYANA* OUTSIDE INDIA

As early as AD 251, K'ang-seng-hui rendered the *Jataka* form of the *Ramayana* into Chinese. In AD 472, another Chinese translation was prepared of the *Nidana* of *Dasharatha Jataka* from a lost Sanskrit text, by Kekaya. In the sixth century, the Simhala poet-king, Kumaradasa, composed the *Janakiharana,* the earliest Sanskrit work of Ceylon. In seventh century Cambodia, Khmer citations attested to the popularity of the *Ramayana.* An inscription declared that a certain Somasharman presented "the *Ramayana,* the *Purana,* and the complete *Bharata*" to a temple. Towards the close of the ninth century, an East Iranian version of the *Ramayana* appeared in Khotanese, an Iranian dialect. The story of Rama spread in the northern-most lands of Asia from Tibet, where it was found in two versions in manuscripts of the seventh-ninth centuries. The oldest manuscript of the *Ramayana* of Valmiki, dated AD 1075, is preserved in Nepal.

RAMA'S STORY RETOLD IN THE REGIONAL LANGUAGES

Somewhere between the ninth and twelfth centuries AD, a Tamil rendition of Rama's story, the *Iramavataram*, "The Descent of Rama," was composed by Kampan, the "emperor of poets." This was the first adaptation in a language other than Sanskrit or Prakrit, and was followed by versions in other languages of the north and south. The Kannada *Pampa Ramayana* was prepared in the eleventh-twelfth century; the Telugu *Ranganatha Ramayanam* in the thirteenth, and a hundred years before Tulsi, Krittivasa, the greatest poet of medieval Bengal, wrote the first *Ramayana* in Bengali. The saint, Ekanatha is remembered for the *Bhavartha Ramayana* in Marathi.

In AD 1574, came Tulsidas's *Ramacharitamanas*, hailed as the greatest epic poem in Hindi. F.S. Growse observed its popularity in 1883, "... the book is in everyone's hands, from the court to the cottage, and is read, or heard, and appreciated alike by every class of the Hindu community, whether high or low, rich or poor, young or old." He said a Hindu who knew only Hindi accepted the *Ramacharitamanas* "as if it were an immemorial *shastra*" (Growse 1914: i-iv). G.A. Grierson wrote, in 1889, "the fact of its universal acceptance by all classes from Bhagalpur to the Punjab and from the Himalaya to the Narmada, is surely worthy of note ... to the vast majority of the people of Hindustan, learned and unlearned alike, their sole norm of conduct is the so-called *Tulsi-krit Ramayana*" (Mehrotra 2006: 50-51). J.N. Farquhar stated, in 1920, that the *Ramacharitamanas* had probably influenced a far greater number of Hindus these last three centuries than any other work. He described Tulsi's work as "the vernacular *Gita*" (Farquhar 1967: 329-30).

8

Hindu Sources on Rama Worship and the Janmabhumi Temple

Left historians describe Rama worship as an eighteenth-nineteenth century phenomena (Jawaharlal Nehru University 1989; Sharma 1990: 24-27). However, from the pre-Christian era onwards sculptural depictions of *Ramayana* themes that were popular among the people had commenced. From the twelfth century AD, temples dedicated exclusively to Rama began to be built.[1]

The oldest of such temples was the one at Ayodhya. Another is at Rajim in Raipur district, which is recorded in the Rajim stone inscription dated AD 1145. It states that king Jagapala (of the Kalachuris of Ratnapur) has "caused this beautiful temple to be constructed for manifesting the splendour of Rama" (*Corpus Inscriptionum Indicarum* Vol. IV Part II: 450-57).

A third documented Rama temple was constructed by Malayasimha, a feudatory of the Kalachuris of Tripuri in AD 1193. An inscription on the temple stated,

> He (i.e. Malayasimha) erected a marvellous row of mansions touching the sky for gods and brahmanas, through fear of

37. The Rajim stone inscription dated AD 1145 recording the construction of a "beautiful temple" for Rama.

> obstruction from which, as it were, the sun's chariot goes obliquely with speed. Having performed fierce and painful penance, the Siddhas go to high heaven, (while) those, who worship (?) at the temple of Rama (built) by him, generally go to the abode of Vishnu (*Corpus Inscriptionum Indicarum* Vol. IV Part I: 346-58).

Several Ramaite cult texts were composed from the eleventh-twelfth centuries. The three oldest were the *Ramapurvatapaniya Upanishad*, the *Ramarakshastotra* of Budhakaushika, and the *Agastya Samhita,* which probably originated in Banaras in the twelfth century and dealt with Shiva's conversion to Rama *bhakti*. According to its theological doctrine, Rama was not just as an incarnation of Vishnu, but the Supreme Reality itself (Bakker I 1986: 67-71). The *Agastya Samhita* is one of the oldest texts to provide details of the ritual worship of Rama (Bakker I 1986: 79-118).

According to Hans Bakker, the growing popularity of Rama worship occurred alongside the spread of an emotional type of *bhakti* in north India in the medieval period in which the cult of the name acquired prominence. The first literary reference to this practice in Vaishnavism was in the *Bhagavata Purana*. By just repeating the four syllables NA-RA-YA-NA, the greatest sinner could attain the path of good fortune.

The first theoretical statement in the *Ramapurvatapaniya Upanishad* was that the *bija* RAMA was the infinite absolute. A second, in the *Agastya Samhita*, added that the mere *japa* or *samkirtana* of the name could atone for all sins. In the thirteenth-fourteenth centuries, this cult developed, especially in the movement of a group of *bhaktas* called *Sants*. The *Sant* movement acquired importance in the backdrop of Muslim rule and the activities of Sufi missionaries like Moinuddin Chishti (Bakker I 1986: 119-20). In fifteenth-sixteenth centuries, Vaishnavism and *Santism* tended to merge, a tendency that found expression in Tulsi's *Ramacharitamanas*. By then, Rama had become the most common word to denote God (Bakker I 1986: 124).

The oldest non-Hindu text to provide a description of the sacred complex at Ayodhya was Jinaprabhasuri's *Tirthakalpa,* dated AD 1332. It referred to the *ghats* on the river Sarayu, Svargadvara and Gopratara, and the Naga sanctuary. Sita Kunda was mentioned among the many Hindu *tirthas, anegani loiatittani* (Bakker I 1986: 125). The prohibition on new temples during the Muslim period may have left the alternative of resorting to holy bathing places in rivers and ponds (Bakker Part II 1986: xvii, 125).

Sridhara, a writer from southern India, in his *Smrtyarthasara,* written in the second half of the twelfth century, mentioned Ayodhya among the *khsetras* that conferred release (*muktiksetrani*) (Kane Vol. I Part II 1997: 725-27).

Hans Bakker has critically examined three main recensions of the *Ayodhya Mahatmya*, the chief work extolling the sacred sites of the holy city and relating them to incidents from the life of Rama.[2]

He has traced the transmission of the text from the twelfth century AD. According to him, a local loose and rudimentary version of the *Ayodhya Mahatmya* as a floating collection of text-fragments bearing on a cluster of holy places was produced in Ayodhya. This was first redacted by the compiler of the *Vaisnavakhanda* of the *Skanda Purana,* and was called *Ayodhya Mahatmya.* This text was worked upon by another author. Still later, a learned pandit of Ayodhya composed a new recension. Throughout, it retained the title *Ayodhya Mahatmya* (Bakker Part II 1986: xxxii).

The location of various temples and sacred sites was given in the *Ayodhya Mahatmya.* Bakker attempted to match them with existing structures,

> ...It is uncertain which places are meant in situation... Unmatta and Lomasa do not occur elsewhere in the Mahatmya, while Vighnesvara (if identified with Vighnesa)

> was said ... to lie south-west of the Janmasthan instead of west... Nowadays a *math* names Ramgulela is believed to represent Lomasa, but this place lies about 350 m east of the Janmasthan ...The given distance of the Kaikeybhavana and Sumitrabhavana (respectively 36 m and 55 m), when reckoned from the mosque of Babur, do not correspond with the modern situation..More difficult to explain is the location of the Janmasthana with respect to Vighnesa...
>
> Notwithstanding all the difficulties discussed above, the original location of the Janma-sthana is comparatively certain since it seems to be attested by the location of the mosque built by Babur, in the building of which materials of a previous Hindu temple were used and are still visible. The mosque is believed by general consensus to occupy the site of the Janmasthana. After the destruction of the original temple a new Janmasthana temple was built on the north side of the mosque separated from it by a street (Bakker Part II 1986: 144-46).

Among other medieval works on Ayodhya was the *Avadha vilasa* of Lal Das, composed in the city in the seventeenth century. It also provided a detailed account of the birthplace of Rama (Bakker 1986: 146).

The sacredness of Ayodhya figured in Sikh literature as well. Guru Nanak's visit to the city was mentioned in several Punjabi works. Bhai Mani Singh's *Pothi Janam Sakhi* (composed in AD 1730) stated that Nanak said to his companion Mardana, *"Mardania! Eh Ajudhia nagari Sri Ramchandra Ji ki hai. So, chal, iska darsan karie."*(Mardana! This Ayodhya city belongs to Sri Ramachandra Ji. Therefore, let us have its *darsana* (Narain 1993:14-15).

END NOTES

1. Hans Bakker noted evidence of the existence of five Vishnu temples in Ayodhya in the twelfth century – Harismrti (Gupta Hari) at the Gopratara *ghat*; Vishnu Hari at the Chakratirtha *ghat*; Chandra Hari on the west side of the

Svargadvara *ghat*; Dharma Hari on the east side of the Svargadvara *ghat*; a Vishnu temple at the Janmabhumi. Three were replaced by mosques, while one was swept away by the Sarayu. The fate of the fifth is unknown but the site is today occupied by a new Gupta Hari/ Chakra Hari temple. During field work he found five Vishnu idols belonging to the eleventh or twelfth century (Bakker I 1986: 54).

2. Hans Bakker referred to an important manuscript of the *Ayodhya Mahatmya* with Jiva Goswami, the well-known disciple of Chaitanya Mahaprabhu,

   "Jiva Gosvami (AD 1523-1608) possessed a M.S. of the A.M. in his library as it is attested by a supposedly autographed hand-list of the titles of texts at his disposal. The list dates from VS 1654 (AD 1597) and comes from the Radha Damodara temple in Vrindaban founded by Jiva Gosvami. It is presently kept in VRI (Vrindavan Research Institute) (Acc. No. 5425)" (Bakker Part II 1986: xvi).

   In "*Ramjanmabhumi-Babri Masjid: A Historians' Report to the Nation*," the four historians, Professors R.S. Sharma, M. Athar Ali, D.N. Jha, and Suraj Bhan had stated,

   "We have used the printed version of the Skanda Purana (Khemraj edn., Bombay, 1910) and two other versions found in manuscript in the Vrindavan Research Institute, Vrindavan, and the Bodleian Library, Oxford. These texts are of recent origin and the insertion of interpolations in the Ayodhya-mahatmya section of the printed Skanda Purana seems to have continued at least till the 18th century. The internal contents of the Skanda Purana including the mention of Vidyapati, who passed away in the first half of the 16th century, show that the core of this Purana was not compiled earlier than the 16th century" (Noorani I 2003: 34).

   Further, they said,

   "The various versions of the Ayodhya-mahatmya seem to have been prepared towards the end of the 18th century or the beginning of the 19th; even as late as that the birthplace was not considered to be important. It is significant that the Janmasthan is not mentioned even once in any itinerary of pilgrimage given in the mahatmya" (Noorani I 2003: 35).

The historians did not specifically mention the MS of *Ayodhya Mahatmya* in the library of Jiva Goswami in AD 1597. Could a four hundred year old manuscript be rightly dubbed "recent"? Kishore Kunal has pointed out that the Left historians appeared to have mistaken Vidyapati of the *Skanda Purana*, a legendary figure, with the famous Maithili poet who had died by the mid-fifteenth century (Kunal 2016: xi, 343).

9

Pillar Bases – the First Archaeological Evidence

The first hint of archaeological evidence of a temple below Babri Masjid was provided in 1988 by Professor B.B. Lal (former Director-General of the Archaeological Survey of India — 1968-1972). Between 1975 and 1980, Professor Lal had undertaken a project, *Archaeology of the Ramayana Sites* (Earlier, in 1969-70, the Department of Ancient Indian History, Culture and Archaeology of the Banaras Hindu University, had conducted excavations at Ayodhya under Professor A.K. Narain). He had selected five sites for investigation — Ayodhya, the capital of the Kosala kingdom and the place of Rama's origin; Sringaverapura, where Rama, Sita, and Lakshmana crossed the Ganga at the commencement of their exile; Bharadvaja Ashram where they stayed overnight and paid their respects to the sage; Chitrakut, where they lived before proceeding southwards; and Nandigram, from where Bharata supervised the affairs of government in Rama's absence.

Professor Lal's initial findings were published in *Indian Archaeology 1976-77 – A Review* (Archaeological Survey of India

1980: 52-53). The excavations had revealed that the first occupation of Ayodhya could be assigned to the early seventh century BC. The Gupta period was not significantly indicated; there was a break in occupation and the site was re-occupied around the eleventh century AD. As the objective of the excavations was to establish the antiquity of the settlement, the brief report was limited to that aspect.

Soon after, in October 1988, a seminar was organized by the Indian Council of Historical Research (ICHR) on "New Archaeology and India." At the seminar, Professor Lal presented a paper, "Historicity of the *Mahabharata* and the *Ramayana*: What has Archaeology to Say in the Matter?" Therein he stated,

> In the Janmabhumi area, the uppermost levels of a trench that lay immediately to the south of the Babri Masjid brought to light a series of brick-built bases which evidently carried pillars thereon. In the construction of the Babri Masjid a few stone pillars had been used, which may have come from the preceding structure.

Kishore Kunal, who in 1990 was appointed Officer on Special Duty (Ayodhya) by Prime Minister, V.P. Singh, met B.B. Lal to enquire about the excavations. B.B. Lal confirmed that the remnants of a temple lay beneath the Masjid. When V.P. Singh was succeeded as Prime Minister by Chandra Shekhar, Kunal informed the latter of his discussion with B.B. Lal. On Chandra Sekhar's request, Lal sent a letter to the Government on 3rd December 1990;

> **A note on the brick-bases of pillars found in the excavations in the Janma-Bhumi area at Ayodhya.**
>
> Under a project called 'Archaeology of the Ramayana Sites' excavations were carried out between 1975 and 1986 at five sites, viz. Ayodhya, Sringaverapura, Bharadvaja Asrama, Chitrakuta and Nandigrama, all associated with that epic.

> At Ayodhya, as many as fourteen trenches were laid out at different spots, one of which was the area known as the Janmabhumi. Over here is a trench hardly three meters to the south of the compound wall of the structure known as Babri Masjid, a series of square brick-bases, running in parallel east-west and north-south rows, were discovered within about 25-30 cm below the surface. Since one row of these pillar bases lay under the edge of the trench towards the compound wall of the mosque, it is likely that there may exist many more such pillar bases in the unexcavated area in that direction. Stratigraphic evidence indicates that these pillar-bases are ascribable to a period around AD 1100. From the level associated with the destruction of these pillar-bases has been found glazed pottery ascribable to fourteenth-fifteenth century AD.
>
> In the mosque there are fourteen stone pillars some of which appear to be in position and oriented east-west and north-south. On the basis of the decorative motifs, sculptures, etc., these pillars are also ascribed to the eleventh century AD. In all probability, the brick-bases found in the excavations and the stone pillars standing in the mosque belong to one and the same structural complex which stood at the site immediately before the Babri Masjid (Kunal 2016: xxxvii).

The mention of pillar bases and their relationship with the pillars in Babri Masjid drew a swift rejoinder from Left historians. In a joint statement, Professors Romila Thapar, S. Gopal, and K.N. Panikkar argued that the fact that pillar bases were running behind the wall surrounding the mosque did not necessarily mean that they ran under the mosque as well. There was space between the wall and mosque, and the pillar bases may well have terminated just behind the wall.

Further, they stated that brick pillar bases did not in themselves indicate the presence of a temple. The structure supported by such a base could have been a brick structure with arches, "the kind of structure common in medieval times, which may have been a hall adjoining a mosque." Also, the decorations on the stone pillars were not exclusive to temple architecture; domestic construction could just as well have had the same decorative motifs. Load-bearing pillars, too, did not mean that they were in exactly the same position as when first used. It was possible to bring pillars from elsewhere and use them as load-bearing pillars in a new construction (*Indian Express* 5.12.1990). Professor S.P. Gupta refuted these all these assertions in a series of articles (*Indian Express* 6.12.1990; 20.12.1990).

On 12th February 199, Professor Habib (then Chairman of ICHR) joined the debate. Delivering a talk at Aligarh Muslim University on "Ayodhya: The National Stake," he vehemently attacked B.B. Lal, the first to point to architectural remnants below Babri Masjid. Professor Habib argued that the existence of pillars in Babri Masjid did not imply that it stood on the site of a temple. It was a common practice to use old pillars not only in mosques, but even in temples. The pillars in the Masjid could well have belonged to a Jain or Shaivite or any other temple, and could not be identified with Rama iconography (*People's Democracy*, 7th and 14th April 1991; *Muslim India*, May 1991).

Meanwhile, the Director General (DG) of ASI, M.C. Joshi in a letter [D.O. letter No. 20/37/90-EE (Part)] dated 2nd May 1991, endorsed the findings of Professors A.K. Narain and B.B. Lal. He wrote,

> Dear Shri Kunal,
>
> Kindly refer to your D.O. letter No. 5602/MOS/91 dated 16th April 1991, regarding the views of Archaeological Survey of India on annexure 28 related to Ramjanambhoomi Babri Masjid dispute.
>
> In this connection I may say that there should not be any doubt to anyone regarding archaeological facts (remains and antiquities) unearthed by Prof. A.K. Narain and Prof. B.B. Lal or about the nature of the structure of Babri Masjid, which though a mosque built in 1528-29 as per the inscribed

> record, shows internally the reuse of earlier carved structurally members including the pillars of pre-13th century AD (dating around circa 11th century AD or so).
>
> The authenticated preliminary report of Prof. Lal, which has already been sent to you vide D.O. letter of the even number dated 11-4-91, explains the purpose of taking up the project called Archaeology of Ramayana Sites by him under which he excavated besides Ayodhya three or four related sites. As the Babri Masjid is not a centrally protected monument, the Archaeological Survey of India has not so far made any detailed study of the monument (Kunal 2016: xxxv-xxxvi).

Prof D.N. Jha then wrote to the Ministry of Home Affairs for access to the archaeological excavations in connection with Ayodhya. On receiving his letter Kishore Kunal asked the DG of ASI to make all relevant material available. The DG replied (D.O. letter no. 20/37/90-EE dated 3rd May 1991),

> Kindly refer to your D.O. letter No. 504/MOS (S)/91 dated 5th February, 1991 forwarding a copy of letter addressed to Shri Subodh Kant Sahay, Minister of State for Home Affairs by Prof. D.N. Jha requesting to supply relevant documents mentioned in the letter.
>
> 2. The matter has been examined at the highest level and it has been decided that the experts may be shown photographs (enclosed) of the controversial trench AVID-4 pertaining to the Ayodhya excavations to clarify the locus of the excavator's findings. Any scholar on the basis of photographs can assess nature of the exposed structure and understand himself the relation between the structures and stratigraphy.
>
> 3. If necessary, thereafter a meeting would be arranged between Prof. B.B. Lal and other scholars holding diverse views on the subject and he would be requested to show the relevant documents in his possession.

4. If this is agreed upon, a meeting would be arranged between the excavator and scholars on a mutually agreed date.
5. Incidentally I may mention for your information that Prof. B.B. Lal is in USA at present.

With regards
Yours sincerely
(MC Joshi)
Encl: two photographs
(Kunal 2016: xl-xli).

This was conveyed to the Left historians, who remained dissatisfied. However, soon after Chandra Shekhar resigned as Prime Minister and there was a break in communications (Kunal 2016: xli).

Kunal regarded it a tragedy that the four historians who claimed to be "an independent forum of historians" took upon themselves the task of passing judgement on all three branches of the evidence – archaeological, archival, and historical (Kunal 2016: xli).

BMAC HISTORIANS *REPORT TO THE NATIONS*

On 13th May 1991, four Left historians — Professors R.S. Sharma, M. Athar Ali, D.N. Jha, and Suraj Bhan released *"Ramjanmabhumi-Babri Masjid: A Historians' Report to the Nation."* They regretted that the Government had begun consultations with the VHP and the BMAC in order to examine the historical and legal merits of the case. This indicated that the Government would serve as umpire in disputes over facts of history. The BMAC historians had, therefore, requested the Government to include "impartial historians" when forming a judgement on historical facts. The Government's response had been "largely one of silence." Nonetheless in "national interest" they had scrutinized the evidence submitted to the Government by the VHP and BMAC and also collected "historical material" on their own. Two of them had even visited Ayodhya to examine the structure and site.

The BMAC historians challenged the VHP claims that the Hindus had long believed that there was a sacred spot in Ayodhya where Lord Rama was born, that a temple dedicated to Rama was built on that site, that it was pulled down on orders of Babur, and that Babri Masjid built in its place. They said the VHP had been unable to cite any ancient Sanskrit text to support its assertions. The only text they had quoted was the *Skanda Purana,* wherein the *Ayodhya Mahatmya* mentioned the merits of visiting Ayodhya. The BMAC historians regarded the *Ayodhya Mahatmya* a late work, full of interpolations. Versions were being prepared even at the close of the eighteenth and beginning of the nineteenth century; "even as late as that the birthplace was not considered to be important." Further, they claimed, the information in the *Ayodhya Mahatmya* on the location of the birthplace did not lead to the Babri Masjid site.

As for the black stone pillars with decorated motifs, the BMAC historians claimed these were not *in situ* and it was entirely possible that they were brought from outside "to decorate" the Masjid (Noorani I 2003: 33-46).

PHOTOGRAPHIC EVIDENCE OF PILLAR BASES

In 1992, a booklet, *Ram Janmabhumi Ayodhya: New Archaeological Discoveries,* (Sharma, Y.D., et al.) published for the first time pictures of pillar bases taken at the time of excavations by B.B. Lal, and preserved in the photo-archives of the Excavation Branch of ASI.

Professor B.B. Lal's findings were examined by the BMAC historians and VHP experts at Purana Qila on 23rd October 1992. At a press conference thereafter, the BMAC historians stated that no fragment of a stone temple had been reported in the relevant trench. They claimed that "the structure found in the trench was undoubtedly an ordinary pillared structure."

The fourteen black stone pillars inside the mosque were "not load-supporting pillars but only decorative pieces as the mosque pillars in which they were embedded were about seven feet wide" (*Indian Express* 24 October 1992; *The Statesman* 24 October 1992; Noorani I 2003: 379-82).

Subsequently, in a press statement on 8th November 1992, the BMAC historians reiterated that the pillar bases had no connection with the pillars standing in the arches of the mosque. The pillar base building was an ordinary structure, "neither religious nor monumental." They added,

> Though we do not deny the possibility of the presence of temples in an ancient city like Ayodhya, despite our frantic and continuous search for the presence of a temple at the Babri site for the last twenty-two months, so far we have not been favoured with any luck (*People's Democracy* 8 November 1992; 15 November 1992).

In his book, *Ayodhya: Archaeology after Demolition*, D. Mandal, a pro-Babri archaeologist, also attempted to disprove B.B. Lal's findings. He dismissed the argument that a "pillared building" was raised in the eleventh century (Mandal 1993: 39-40). Subsequently, during examination by the Allahabad High Court, Mandal confessed that his book was based "chiefly" on the photograph taken by Prof. B.B. Lal near Babri Masjid. The Court felt constrained to observe,

> Only on that basis, he (Mandal) wrote a book, and analyzed the belief of the people whether the disputed structure was constructed after demolishing a temple or that there existed any temple of 11th or 12th century which was demolished before its construction.

The Court said,

> the entire opinion of this witness is short of the requirement under Section 45 of the Evidence Act 1872 to qualify as an Expert ... (page 3655 para 3629).

D. Mandal, as per Court records, "is not a Ph. D but many have been awarded Ph. D under his guidance" (page 696 para 485). He is also a card holding member of the Communist Party (page 3648 para 3628). The Court noted that though Mandal tried to counter B.B. Lal, he,

> could not dispute the existence of some structure beneath the disputed structure but refuted the claim that it was a massive temple of 11th or 12th century and instead suggested that it could have been structure of 13th to 15th century (pages 3708-09 para 3650).

The Court also observed that Shereen Ratnagar, who wrote the introduction to Mandal's book, tried to give "justification to a report or comments of a person, who himself had not gone into field archaeology" (page 3705 para 3647). Shereen Ratnagar was constrained to admit in Court,

> It is substantially correct that I wrote my critique on the basis of the said sole photograph (by B.B. Lal) (page 4033 para 3854). ... some sketches ... given in my Introduction ... are purely ... hypothetical (page 4033 para 3853). ... in India I have not done any digging and excavation on my own (page 4033 para 3852).

10

A Gahadavala Inscription Recovered and Treta Ka Thakur Re-discovered

An added definitive proof that a temple lay beneath Babri Masjid came with the discovery of an inscription, on a stone slab approximately 5 feet by 2.25 feet, during the demolition of 6th December 1992. Dr. K.V. Ramesh, renowned epigraphist and former Director of Epigraphy, ASI, was directed by the High Court to decipher the inscription and provide a comprehensive translation (pages 3688-97 para 3636).

In a report submitted alongside, K.V. Ramesh noted that the subjoined stone inscription was engraved on a rectangular slab, the written area roughly covering a space 115 cm x 55 cm. The inscription was of twenty lines. The slab, as extant, was diagonally broken in two, resulting in the loss of a few letters in almost every line. It was written in "fairly chaste Sanskrit." Ramesh dated it to the mid-twelfth century AD on paleographical grounds, as well as the internal evidence provided by the inscription. The most important historical information he found was the mention of King

Govindachandra, obviously of the Gahadavala dynasty, who ruled over a fairly vast empire from AD 1114 to AD 1155.

Verse 1 was entirely lost. The badly damaged second verse invoked Lord Trivikrama, so appeared composed in praise of Vishnu. Verse 3, also mutilated, seemed to refer to the destruction of the warrior clans by Bhargava-Parashurama. Verse 4 mentioned the rise of a Kshatriya family, heroes born in which resurrected the warrior clans. Verse 5 stated that in that noble family was born the beloved of the people, Mame. Verse 7 spoke of his detachment from mundane things. Verse 8 said that he bequeathed his kingdom and wealth to his son, Sallaksana. Verses 9 to 14 contained praises of Sallaksana. Verse 15 mentioned the birth of his son, who bore a striking resemblance to the father. Verse 16 referred to this son as Alhana and stated that he revived the past power and glory of his family. Verses 17 and 18 contained praises of him. Verse 19 stated that his nephew, Meghasuta, superseded a certain Anayacandra and obtained the Lordship of Saketa-mandala through the grace of the senior lord of the earth, Govindachandra. Verse 20 lauded the military might of this hero. Verse 21 noted that in order to ensure his easy passage into the heavens, Meghasuta built a lofty stone temple for the God, Vishnu Hari. Verse 22 stated that he, who was responsible for the stability of Govindachandra's empire, was succeeded by the younger Ayusyacandra as the lord of Saketa-mandala (subsequently K.V. Ramesh modified this to read "Ayusyacandra, son of Alhana occupied the position of Meghasuta as chief of Saketa mandala"). Verse 23 contained conventional praise of Ayusyacandra. According to Verse 24, he set up residence in the city of Ayodhya, which was adorned with lofty abodes, intellectuals and temples, and added to the entire Saketa mandala thousands of small and big reservoirs. Verses 25 and 26 were devoted to more conventional praises of Ayusyacandra. Verse 27, partly damaged, alluded to the well-known episodes of Vishnu's

38. The Treta ka Thakur inscription.

39. The Vishnu Hari inscription recovered in the aftermath of 6th December 1992.

incarnation as Narasimha, Krishna, Vamana and Rama. Verse 28, badly defaced, alluded to the fierce arms of a ruler, probably, Ayusyacandra, that "annihilates even the fear caused by the western (i.e., the Islamic invaders from the west)" forces. The incomplete Verse 29 mentioned King Ayusyacandra (*Puratattva* Number 33, 2002-2003: 98-103).

The reference to Saketa *mandala* was interesting. Ramesh noted that it was well known that North India, like the South, was divided into administrative divisions called *mandalas* (pages 3697-3700 para 3637). He stated that the temple referred to was built by Meghasuta, but the inscription was inscribed later by his successor (pages 3702-03 para 3639). Ramesh's reading of the inscription was accepted by the Allahabad High Court. But that did not settle the matter.

SHIFTING STANCE OF LEFT HISTORIANS

Left historians and archaeologists questioned the genuineness of the inscription. In a paper presented at a seminar of the Association for the Study of History and Archaeology, in Calcutta, in February 1999, D. Mandal pronounced, the inscription "may or may not be fake. However, its provenance is definitely not the walls of the Babri Masjid as claimed." He said, "If it is a genuine inscription, and if the information as contained therein is correctly interpreted, in that case, the temple as referred to should be looked for somewhere else, as there was no temple at the site of the Babri Masjid in Ayodhya ..." (*New Age*, 11-17 April 1999). Mandal offered absolutely no explanation for this analysis.

No less baffling was the opinion of Sita Ram Roy, who dated the inscription to the eighteenth century (Roy 1996: 118-19). He said that the occurrence of the name Ayodhya in the inscription led one to "unhesitatingly ascribe the epigraph to a date posterior to the epic of Tulsidas." For, though the *Ramacharitamanas* mentioned Avadha or Kosala, it did not refer to Ayodhya. The reference to Vishnu Hari also made the epigraph "quite late," as the name Vishnu Hari did not figure in the *Vishnu Sahasranama* found in the *Mahabharata*, the *Padma Purana*, or Shankara's commentary on the thousand names of Vishnu. Sita Ram Roy stated that the term Vishnu Hari did not connote Lord Vishnu, "rather it signifies an individual person, named Vishnu Hari." Roy speculated that the term *mandira* found in the inscription "originally and usually means a dwelling house, particularly a palace. It would be the mansion of king (sic), named Vishnuhari" (Roy 1996: 119).

In his deposition before the Allahabad High Court, K.V. Ramesh declared it incorrect that till the thirteenth century the word *devalaya*, not *mandir*, was used for a temple. It was also wrong to say that till the twelfth century, *mandir* denoted human dwellings, not temples (pages 3702-03 para 3639).

It is noteworthy that the *Ayodhya Mahatmya* mentioned seven "*Hars*" or representations of Vishnu on the banks of river Saryu — Gupt Har, Chandra Har, Chakra Har, Vishnu Har, Dharma Har, Belma Har, and Pun Har (page 4676).

Shockingly, Sita Ram Roy subsequently admitted in Court that at the time of writing his article he had "not seen full photograph, estampage of the inscription or its decipherment" (page 4036 para 3858). Yet he had no qualms in pontificating on a matter of such importance in the Ayodhya dispute.

His viewpoint had its share of supporters. Dr. K. M. Shrimali of Delhi University, while dismissing as "some-what childish" the suggestion that stone inscriptions could be forged, added a warning note,

> The capabilities of modern-day stone cutters and carvers should neither be underestimated nor denied. It is well known that the renowned family of the Sompuras, specializing in stone engravings and sculptural art for over a millennium, has been entrusted the task of building the 'grand temple of Lord Rama' at Ayodhya ...

He also agreed with Sita Ram Roy's dating of the inscription (Noorani I 2003: 81).

The most sustained campaign against the inscription was mounted by Professor Irfan Habib. In an article in *People's Democracy,* on 8th December 2002, Professor Habib declared that the inscription was "certainly a plant as far as the mosque is concerned." He rejected the statements of witnesses that the stone slab came from the thick outer wall, which comprised two walls enclosed with a large amount of rubble mixed with lime mortar and explained why it was covered with mortar when it fell. He alleged that the inscription must have come "from some private collection," and definitely not from the Babri Masjid.

He conceded that the inscription did not appear a forgery and could paleographically be placed "within a long period, eleventh to fourteenth centuries." Further, "The word *mandira* used for a temple (and not, as in earlier inscriptions, for a court) suggested a late rather than an earlier date." But even if it was ascribed to the twelfth century at Ayodhya (for which it used the name Saketa), it did not validate the VHP claim that a Janmabhumi temple stood at the site. Describing K.V. Ramesh as "a VHP witness" but an epigraphist of repute, Professor Habib asserted that, as per the inscription, the temple "was not important enough" to involve the Gahadavala king, Govindachandra, himself.

Professor Habib also faulted Ramesh's translation of the word *"pashchayats"* that occurred in Lines 19-20 of the inscription. Ramesh had translated this as, "And now, the fierce arms of the ruler... annihilates even the fear caused by the westerners (*pashchatyas*)." He viewed this as a reference to Muslims, especially the Ghaznavids. Professor Habib, however, argued that the word *'pashchatyas'* had never been used for Muslims and Ghaznavids in any inscription or Sanskrit text. It could, instead, be a reference to the Rashtrakutas of Kanauj and Badaun, who were the western neighbours of the Gahadavalas in the first half of the twelfth century. Also, *'pashchatya'* normally meant one coming in the future, "so that the ruler praised was really warding off future dangers and not any current 'western' enemies" (Noorani I 2003: 127-28).

Irrespective of the merits of Professor Habib's interpretation of the word *'pashchatyas,'* the Gahadavalas from the outset certainly stood forth as champions of Hindu *dharma*. Chandradeva, the founder of the dynasty, is described in one of the records as "Svayambhu himself born upon the earth to restore *dharma* and the Veda, whose sounds had almost been silenced" (Pollock 1994: 106). The copper plate grant of his son and grandson, Madanapala and Govindachandra, of Vikram year 1154 (AD 1097), also recorded that Chandradeva had protected Kashi, Kusika or Kanyakubja, Uttara Kosala or Ayodhya, and the city of Indra (*The Indian Antiquary* 18: 11, 13). The Machchlishahr copper plate inscription (AD 1197), issued by the last ruler of the Gahadavala dynasty, noted that Chandradeva had been the protector of the holy places, Kashi, Kusika, Uttara Kosala, and Indrasthaniyaka (Prasad 1990: 58-56).

King Govindachandra, was described by Lakshmidhara, author of the *Krtyakalpataru*, as one "who killed in battle, the heroic Hammira ...," a reference to a Muslim chief, possibly Hajib Tugha-tigin (Niyogi 1959: 57-58, 60). The copper-plate grant of Madanapala and Govindachandra, of Vikram year 1166, also extolled his "matchless fighting (which) makes the Hammira lay aside (his) enmity" (*The Indian Antiquary* 18: 16, 18). At Sarnath, near Varanasi, an inscription of Kumara Devi, the queen of Govindachandra, compared him to Vishnu, reborn to defend his realm. It stated,

> Hari (Vishnu), who had been commissioned by Hara (Siva), in order to protect Varanasi from the wicked Turushka warrior, as the only one who was able to protect the earth, was again born from him, his name being renowned as Govindachandra — *Varanasim bhuvana-raksana-daksah dustat Turuska-subhata-davitum ...* (*Epigraphia Indica* IX: 337).

Within half a century of the death of Mahmud Ghaznavi, the Gahadavalas had initiated a major building programme at Ayodhya. Among the temples they built were the Chandra Hari, Vishnu Hari, and Dharma Hari temples. Govindachandra had also sponsored a massive fourteen-volume compendium of social/religious codes of conduct, the *Krtyakalpataru*, in recognition of the need "for special reaffirmation of *dharma*," at a time when it faced in the Turks "a resolutely unassimilating social and religious formation" (Pollock 1994: 105-06).

Be that as it may, Professor Habib summed up his views on the inscription,

> We are thus left with an inscription brought from somewhere else, which merely says that a local lord of Saketa, among other things, built a beautiful temple for Vishnu-Hari. This was not built at the birth-site of Lord Rama, nor at the site of any earlier temple... There is no certainty at all ... that the inscribed slab was intended to be placed in the temple, the reference to which occupies only one out of its twenty legible verses. The inscription, finally, has no reference at all to any Muslim danger or any earlier temple having been destroyed by Muslims...As for the Babri Masjid having been built at the site of *any* temple, let us now remember that all the archaeological evidence adduced by VHP is heavily tainted.

In the above article written in 2002, Professor Habib had claimed that the inscription must have come "from some private collection." At the Indian History Congress in 2006, he modified his hypothesis and proclaimed it had been "surreptitiously removed from the Lucknow Museum and paraded off as a find from the Babri Masjid."

Professor Habib now modified his position to claim that the colonial archaeologist, A. Fuhrer, had found an inscription at the Treta Ka Thakur temple in Ayodhya and placed it in the Faizabad Museum. The inscription was later shifted to Lucknow Museum from where it "has mysteriously disappeared." The missing inscription, according to Professor

Habib precisely matched the one planted at Ayodhya (Habib 2007: 359-60).

Fuhrer had mentioned an inscription he found at the Treta ka Thakur, in his *The Sharqi Architecture of Jaunpur,*

> Inscription No. XLIV is written in twenty incomplete lines on a white sandstone, broken off at either end, and split in two parts in the middle. It is dated samvat 1241, or AD 1184, in the time of Jayachandra of Kanauj, whose praises it records for erecting a Vaishnava temple, from whence this stone was originally brought and appropriated by Aurangzib in building his masjid known as Treta ki (sic) Thakur. The original slab was discovered in the ruins of this Masjid, and is now in the Faizabad local Museum (Fuhrer 1889: 68).

Fuhrer described the inscription again in *The Monumental Antiquities And Inscriptions In The North-Western Provinces And Audh,*

> A fragmentary inscription of Jayachandra of Kanauj, dated samvat 1241, and recording the erection of temple of Vishnu was rescued from the ruins of Aurangzeb's Masjid, known as Treta-ka-Thakur, and is now in the Faizabad Museum (Fuhrer II 1891: 297).

Professor Habib maintained that it was possible Fuhrer "merely assumed from the date Sam. 1241/1184 AD that the inscription referred to Jayachandra, the Gahadavala ruler, who ruled from AD 1170 to 1194, without actually finding the name recorded in the inscription" (Habib 2007: 359).

Irfan Habib cited the work of Hans Bakker, who had stated that Fuhrer's inscription was preserved at Lucknow Museum (where it was listed as Arch. Dep. 53.4) and had never been published (Bakker I 1986: 52).

He also referred to Dr. Jahnawi Roy, who had examined an inscription bearing number 53.4 at Lucknow Museum. It was 2'8" in length and 10" in width and made no mention of

Jayachandra (Roy 1994: 114-16). Professor Habib additionally mentioned a paper by Dr. Pushpa Prasad, who claimed that the inscription at Lucknow Museum was actually two largely illegible texts on two unrelated stone blocks, one with a text of Gahadavala link, the other paleographically of Chandella origin (Prasad 2004: 348-50).

According to Professor Habib that these findings made it clear that the original twenty-line Treta-ka-Thakur inscription was removed from Lucknow Museum and replaced by two totally unrelated illegible blocks "so as to make up twenty lines, the same number of lines on the inscription that was recorded by Fuhrer." The slab, purportedly found at the Babri Masjid site, broken vertically in the middle, "precisely matches" Fuhrer's inscription. The bottom part "where the date should have come seems to have been deliberately broken off," perhaps "to ward off suspicions about its being the same as the Fuhrer-discovered inscription" (Habib 2007: 359-60).

In an article in the *People's Democracy*, on 17th October 2010, soon after the Allahabad High Court had delivered its judgement, Professor Habib again called the inscription "a plant" (Sahmat 2010a: 48). In a pamphlet issued around the same time by the Aligarh Historians Society and edited by him, Professor Habib noted that the "strong evidence in relation to the Vishnu-Hari temple inscription, of theft, manipulation and misrepresentation on the part of the VHP" had been "passed over in silence"[1] (Sahmat 2010b: 36).

THE DENOUEMENT

A counter to the many conjectures of Dr. Jahnawi Roy, Dr. Pushpa Prasad, and above all, Professor Irfan Habib has been provided by Kishore Kunal. He has published, perhaps for the first time, a photograph of the Treta Ka Thakur inscription lodged in Lucknow Museum (inscription No. 53.4). Dr. Roy's statement that the inscription is in ten lines (Roy 1994: 114-16) is shown to be wholly wrong. Even a visual inspection reveals that the inscription is of twenty lines. Though the inscription is broken in the middle, the two parts are in vertical continuation; "the angles of the broken lower portion and the upper portion of the two parts are almost the same and even the broken letters of both the portions match each other" (Kunal 2016: 304-05).

Kishore Kunal also checked the Annual Report of Lucknow Museum (April 1950-March 1954). On page 63, inscription 53.4 was clearly described as having 20 lines (not 10 as claimed by Dr. Roy). It was broken in the middle and the top, was on white sandstone, and measured 2′4" in length and 10.5" in breadth (Kunal 2016: 307). This entry in the Annual Report of Lucknow Museum (April 1950-March 1954) precisely matches the Treta ka Thakur inscription (no. 53.4) in the Museum. The entry also clearly states that the inscription came from Faizabad Museum.

Pushpa Prasad's assertion that "the purported single inscription is actually an assemblage of two different inscriptions, each incomplete" was also found to be inaccurate. The two parts, when put together "show that the broken letters are continuous on both parts." This establishes that both parts are complementary to each other; "they are parts of the same inscription without any doubt." There was nothing to support Pushpa Prasad's statement that one part belonged to the Gahadawala dynasty and the other to the Chandella dynasty. Further, her claim that the inscription related to a land grant was not substantiated. The inscription being badly damaged does not convey any "concrete meaning" (Kunal 2016: 307-10, 312-33).

Thus far neither Dr. Roy, nor Professor Prasad, nor Professor Irfan Habib have responded to the publication of the photograph of the Treta Ka Thakur inscription, which falsifies the arguments they have been persistently advocating for over two decades.

END NOTES

1. Equally intriguing seems to be the story of the inscriptions on the walls of Babri Masjid. Muhammad Asghar, in a counter affidavit filed on 22nd December 1885 against a suit by Raghubar Das, mentioned one inscription. He stated that when Badshah Babur had the mosque built, he had the word "Allah" engraved on its door and hence no one else could claim ownership of the building (pages 1143-44 para 827; page 1146 para 832).

   District Judge Col. FEA Chamier in his judgement on 18/26 March 1886 also referred to this one inscription. He noted, "The entrance to the enclosure is under a gateway which bears the superscription 'Allah'..." (Noorani I 2003: 183).

   Francis Buchanan (1762-1829), Scottish physician, surveyor, and botanist, who surveyed Gorakhpur Division for the East India Company in 1813-14, mentioned one inscription in his Report.

   Archaeologist A. Fuhrer during his visit to the site in 1889 found two inscriptions (besides one bearing the *Kalma*). The date of the construction of the mosque in the inscription he saw above the entrance door was AH 930 (AD 1523), which was well before Babur's conquest of India. The name of the builder was Mir Khan, not Mir Baqi.

   Maulvi Shuaib in the *Annual Report of the Office of the Archaeological Surveyor, Northern Circle, Agra*, submitted in 1906 recorded three inscriptions. He saw the inscription mentioned by Fuhrer bearing the date AH 930 (i.e. 1523), but its location appeared to have changed. Appendix D of this Report referred to the inscriptions that were copied at that time. These were listed from serial numbers 10 to 12.

   No. 10 - the stone slab on the outside of the central arch of the Masjid. It was in Persian, named Babur as the ruler, and gave AH 935 i.e. AD 1528 as the date of construction. In the last column under Remarks was written -

   "Records the erection of the mosque which was built on the same spot where the old temple of Janam Asthanam of Ram Chandra was."

No. 11 - the stone slab on the inside of the central arch of the mosque. The ruler named was Babur and the date of construction AH 935 i.e. AD 1528. In the Remarks column was written - "contains sacred words (*Kalmah*)."

No. 12 – the stone slab below the pulpit of the mosque. The ruler mentioned was Babur and the date of construction AH 930 i.e. AD 1523. In the Remarks column it was stated -"The date of its erection is given in a chronogram" (Kunal 2016: 171-73).

The texts of two inscriptions supplied to A.S. Beveridge in 1921 (almost 32 years after Fuhrer) by the Deputy Commissioner of Faizabad appeared to be different from those seen by Fuhrer.

The two inscriptions near the pulpit of the mosque were taken away by rioters in the 1934 riots. One inscription restored by the Muslim community mentioned the date of the construction as AH 923, i.e. AD 1516-17.

Dr. ZA Desai, Superintendent, Persian and Arabic Inscriptions, Nagpur, published an article in *Epigraphia Indica, Arabic and Persian Supplement,* 1965. The original was written by the late Maulvi M Ashraf Husain. In his brief introduction Desai stated that the article was found in the papers of his predecessor with a note that it could be published, after revision, by his successor. Desai stated that he was publishing the article after incorporating new material, but did not specify the material he had added.

He seemed to have arbitrarily changed the text and translation in the name of his predecessor, in a bid to rectify the blunders committed earlier to strengthen the claims of the Sunni Waqf Board to the mosque. Among other alterations, he changed the date from AH 930 (1523) to AH 935 (1528).

The two inscriptions restored by the Muslim community after the riots of 1934 were examined by the Civil Judge, Faizabad in the Regular Suit no. 29 of 1945. The date of the construction of the Masjid was given as AH 923, i.e. AD 1516-17. In one inscription, Mir Baqi was named and shown as a native of Isphahan in Iran. Could this be an attempt to prove he was a Shia, for the *Babur Nama* mentioned him as a Tashkindi? (Kunal 2016: lli-liv; 143-92).

It has been suggested that the inscriptions on Babri Masjid were fixed well after its construction and tampered with several times (Kunal 2016: 143-92). It is a matter of regret that Professor Irfan Habib did not throw any light on this vexatious matter when he expended so much energy on the Vishnu Hari inscription.

11

Left Historians and the ASI Report

The Special (Lucknow) Bench of the Allahabad High Court (comprising Justices Sudhir Narain, S.R. Alam and Bhanwar Singh), directed the Archaeological Survey of India on 5th March 2003 to undertake excavations at Ramjanmabhumi/Babri Masjid to determine "whether there was any temple/structure which was demolished and mosque constructed on the disputed site" (Noorani I 2003: 135-39). The Court was of the view that archaeological evidence would facilitate in resolution of the issue.

ASI CONDUCTS EXCAVATIONS

As per the High Court order, the ASI carried out excavations at the site between 12th March and 7th August 2003 on the basis of a preliminary Ground Penetrating Radar (GPR) survey of the area by Tojo-Vikas International Pvt. Ltd. The GPR survey had revealed numerous anomalies possibly associated with ancient structures, the precise nature of which could be established by archaeological trenching (*Ayodhya: 2002-03*, Vol. I: ASI 2003: 3-5).

The ASI submitted its Report to the Court on 22nd September 2003. In his introductory remarks, Dr. B.R. Mani, Superintending Archaeologist, ASI, and Team Leader, explained the methodology adopted in view of the "limited but defined objective" set by the Court and the time frame within which the work was required to be completed. The latest techniques of layout of trenches were adopted. The entire process of excavation and recording of structures and antiquities was documented by still and video cameras (*Ayodhya: 2002-03*, Vol. I: ASI 2003: 8-9). The main findings of the ASI were:

The site was first occupied by Northern Black Polished Ware (NBPW)-using people in the first millennium BC (Period I). The level yielded pottery, broken weights, fragments of votive tanks, glass beads, discs, broken animal figurine, an iron knife, and a round bezel in greenish glass with the legend "*sidhe*" in high relief in Ashokan Brahmi on the obverse, the reverse being plain (*Ayodhya: 2002-03*, Vol. I: ASI 2003: 38).

The next cultural occupation dated to the Shunga period (second-first century BC; Period II), when the site witnessed the first structural activity in stone and brick. The level was represented by terracotta objects comprising human and animal figurines, a saddle quern, a part of a lid in stone, bangle fragments, and a broken sealing with the "*sa*" letter in Brahmi (*Ayodhya: 2002-03*, Vol. I: ASI 2003: 38-39).

The Kushan period (first to third century AD; Period III) was rich in pottery typical of the era. A huge kiln was noticed, besides animal and human figurines, bangle fragments, a portion of a votive tank, all in terracotta, a hairpin in bone, and an antimony rod in copper. A massive brick construction was noticed, attesting to a spurt in the construction of large structures. From this period, stone and brick constructions were manifest at the site (*Ayodhya: 2002-03*, Vol. I: ASI 2003: 39).

The advent of the Guptas (fourth to sixth century AD; Period IV) did not bring any qualitative change in building activity. Typical terracotta figurines of the period and a copper coin bearing the image of a king on the observe and a *garuda* with the legend *Sri Chandra* (*Gupta*) on the reverse, as well as illustrative potsherds were represented at the site (*Ayodhya: 2002-03,* Vol. I: ASI 2003: 39-40).

From the post-Gupta – Rajput period (seventh to tenth century; Period V), knife-edge bowls and a circular brick shrine, with an entrance from the east, were found. The structure was damaged, but its northern wall still retained provision for a *pranala,* i.e., a water chute, a distinct feature of contemporary temples in the Ganga-Yamuna plain (*Ayodhya: 2002-03,* Vol. I: ASI 2003: 40, 269).

During the early medieval period (11th-12th century AD; Period VI), the remains of a huge structure, nearly 50 m in north-south orientation, were unearthed. A thick floor made of brick crush appeared, on circumstantial evidence, to have been attached to a wide and massive looking brick wall oriented north-south and markedly inclined to the east (Wall No. 17). The structure appeared to have been short-lived, as only four of the fifty pillar bases exposed during the excavations belonged to this level. A fragmentary inscription with a few letters engraved on a red stone slab, dated paleographically to the eleventh century, was also discovered (*Ayodhya: 2002-03,* Vol. I: ASI 2003: 40-41, 204-05, 269).

On the remains of the above structure, a massive structure was constructed (Period VII, twelfth to sixteenth centuries), with at least three structural phases (A, B, and C) and three successive floors attached with it. In phase A, a massive wall (Wall No. 16), nearly 50 m long, in north-south orientation was constructed, the foundation trench of which cut the red brick crush floor of the previous period. A new style of construction was noted in this period in a limited area. A floor of lime mixed with fine clay and brick crush was laid, over

40. Glazed ware sherds.

41. Glazed ware large bowl.

42. Porcelain ware sherds.

43. Terracotta glazed ware sherds.

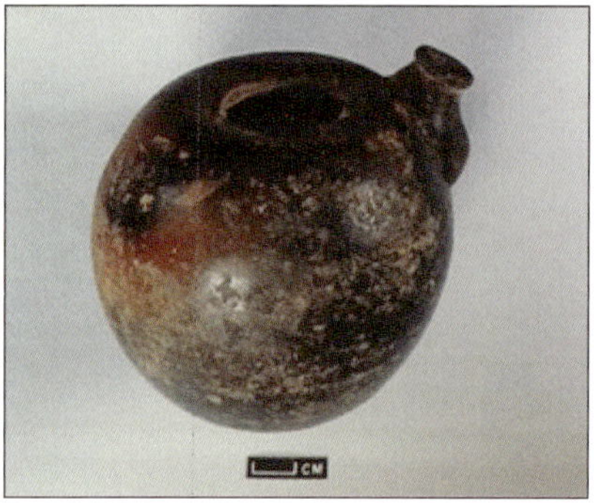

44. Sprouted pot.

46. Leg portion resting on pedestal.

45. Pots from Kushan period.

48. Torso of human figure wearing uttariya, terracotta.

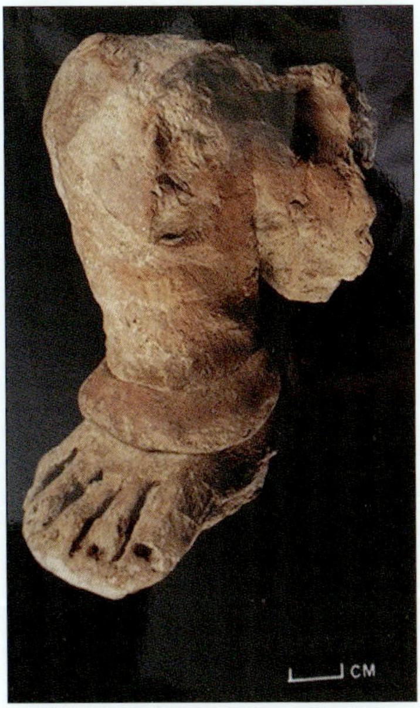

47. A human leg, terracotta.

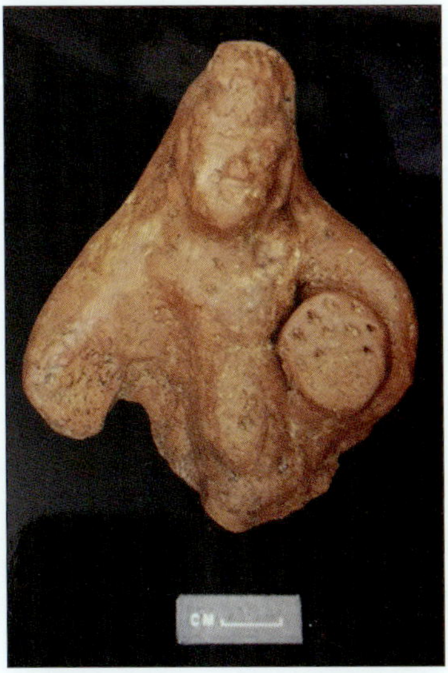

49. Male holding a perforated disc, terracotta.

50. A decorated human head, terracotta.

51. Human head with large earrings, terracotta.

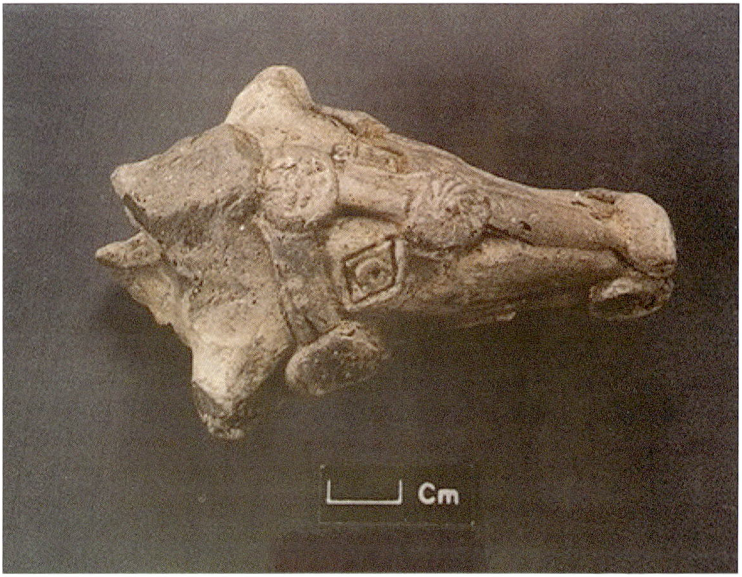

52. Animal head.

53. General view of the excavated trenches in the southern area.

54. North-south oriented brick wall with plastered inner face.

55. Wall of the temple with decorated architectural members.

56. Pillar bases attached to the contemporary floor 2 in northern area.

57. Circular shrine.

58. Tank like structure below Rama Chabutra.

59. Close up of *Makara-pranala* used in wall of the mosque.

61. *Ghata*-shaped pit cut into large brick paving.

60. Some of the decorated 14 stone black pillars used in Babri Masjid.

which a column-based structure was built (evidence of pillar bases were available in some trenches). This floor was traced within a thin walled enclosed area. In phase B, the enclosed area was filled with earth and overlaid with a brickbat paving on top of which a thick floor of lime mixed with grit and fine brick nodules was laid, which ran over the broken/levelled wall. In phase C, foundations to support pillars or columns were sunk. They were overlaid with a 4-5 cm thick floor, which had a grid of square sandstone bases for pillars projecting out, a few of which survive. The floor around most of the pillar bases was found broken, with pillar base foundations in a very disturbed condition.

This massive structure had a minimum dimension of 50 x 30 m in north-south and east-west directions respectively. The architectural members of the earlier short-lived structure, with stencil-cut foliage pattern and other decorative motifs, were reused in the construction of the monumental structure, which had a huge pillared hall (or two halls).

Nearly fifty pillar bases with brickbat foundations, below concrete blocks topped by sandstone blocks were found. From the excavations, it could be inferred that there were seventeen rows of pillar bases from north to south, each row having five pillar bases. Of fifty excavated pillar bases only twelve were completely exposed, thirty-five partially exposed, and three could be traced in sections only. Pillar bases in the central part could not be located due to the presence of Rama *Lalla* at the spot in the make-shift temple.

This massive structure was different from residential structures and provided sufficient evidence of a construction for public usage. It remained in existence for a long time during Period VII (*Ayodhya: 2002-03*, Vol. I: ASI 2003: 41-43, 54-70, 269-70).

It was over this massive structure that Babri Masjid was constructed in the sixteenth century (Period VIII) (*Ayodhya: 2002-03*, Vol. I: ASI 2003: 51-54). The centre of the central chamber of Babri Masjid fell just over the central point of Wall 16 of the preceding massive structure. Towards the east of this central point, a circular depression with projection on the west cut into the large-sized brick pavement, signifying a place where some important object was placed (most likely an image of Garuda).

In the last phase of Period VII, glazed ware shards made their appearance and continued in the succeeding levels of the next periods, where they were accompanied by glazed tiles. These were probably used in the construction of Babri Masjid. This was also true of celadon and porcelain shards recovered in much less quantity. Animal bones were found at various levels of different periods, but skeletal remains noticed in the trenches in northern and southern areas belonged to Period IX (late and post-Mughal level).

The site had also proved significant for taking back its antiquarian remains to the middle of the 13th century BC, on the analogy of the C14 dates (*Ayodhya: 2002-03*, Vol. I: ASI 2003: 270-72). (K.N. Dikshit, who was part of B.B. Lal's team that had earlier excavated at Ayodhya, stressed that the C14 dates supplied by the Birbal Sahani Institute of Palaeobotany, Lucknow, had given a new interpretation to the chronology of the lowest levels. The pre-NBPW deposit had strengthened the Hindu belief that the story of Rama and Ayodhya was earlier than that of Lord Krishna and Hastinapur; *Puratattva* Number 33, 2002-2003: 117).

The ASI Report concluded that, "viewing in totality and taking into account the archaeological evidence of a massive structure just below the disputed structure and evidence of continuity in structural phases from the tenth century onwards up to the construction of the disputed structure along with the yield of stone and decorated bricks as well as mutilated sculpture of divine couple and carved architectural members including foliage patterns, *amalaka*, doorjamb with semi-circular pilaster, broken octagonal shaft of black schist pillar, lotus motif, circular shrine having *pranala* (water chute) in the north, fifty pillar bases in association of the huge structure, are indicative remains which are distinctive features found associated with the temples of north India" (*Ayodhya: 2002-03*, Vol. I: ASI 2003: 272).

Plainly stated, the ASI Report conclusively established that Babri Masjid was not built on virgin land and that the remains found at the site were of religious structures. Wall 5 of the northern chamber of Babri Masjid was raised directly over the western wall (W 16) of the temple without any layer of earth or other strata between the two walls. Wall 5 had no foundation trench. There was not a centimetre of wind or water borne deposit between Wall 5 and Wall 16. In the core of Wall 5, the bricks used for filling were those collected from the demolished temple.

The southern foundation wall (Wall 6) of the Masjid rested directly over two pillar bases of the earlier period below its middle and south-eastern corner. Wall 6 directly abutted with Wall 16. It was clearly visible that the niche of Wall 16 had been blocked by the same size bricks of Wall 16. In the non-blocked area, that is, in the original wall there was a 2 cm thick plaster of lime, which showed that the series of niches in Wall 16 were blocked after demolishing the temple and before raising the mosque. The niches were for the installation of minor deities (*Ayodhya: 2002-03*, Vol. I: ASI 2003: 51-54; Sharma 2011: 31). Wall 7 of Babri Masjid in front of its southern chamber rested over three pillar bases of the earlier period, which were attached through Floor 2 to Wall 16. In other words, the excavations revealed that Babri Masjid was erected over, and with full knowledge of a pre-existing structure.

The continuous nature of the 10.80 m thick deposit, due to the nine cultural periods, indicated that the site was never abandoned and never used for habitational purposes. Four working floors were exposed at the site. The carbon dating for Floor 3, which was below Floor 2, revealed a calibrated age range from AD 900 to 1030. Floor 2, with which the fifty pillar bases were associated, was evidently the floor of the temple. Over Floor 2 was Floor 1, the floor of the Masjid.

The evidence of the existence of a temple at the time of the construction of Babri Masjid was also clear from the plan of the structural remains. These showed the *garbha griha* (where Ram *Lalla* was presently situated), the *ardha mandapa* and the wide *mandapa*, along with the *pushkarani* on the north-east corner, the wide walls and damaged structural parts of earlier temples and religious members of the last temple were used in the walls of the mosque (Sharma 2011: 38).

SUNNI CENTRAL WAQF BOARD – LEFT HISTORIANS ATTACK ASI

Both during and after the excavations, pro-Babri group carried out a well coordinated campaign to discredit the ASI, within and outside the Court. The dramatis personae included the eight archaeologists presented as experts in excavations by the Sunni Central Waqf Board in Court, and Left historians led by Professor Irfan Habib outside. The eight archeologists were Suraj Bhan, D. Mandal, Jaya Menon, Supriya Verma, Ashok Dutta, Shereen Ratnagar, Sita Ram Roy, and R.C. Thakran. The objections raised by pro-Babri archeologists, during the course of excavations and on cross-examination in Court, were remarkably similar to the protestations of Professor Irfan Habib. The same points were raised, often in the same language. The views of both must be regarded as a joint attack on the Report.

Professor Habib's critique came even before the final Report had been submitted to the Court. In an article in the *Hindustan Times*, on 6th July 2003, he asked whether the ASI would "simply set its sights at finding what those in power wish it to find: the remains of a temple?" He accused the ASI of deliberately overlooking material evidence that pointed to the existence of an earlier mosque below Babri Masjid! On the pillar bases, he said, "they could just be low seats or, in some cases, markers for shops or stalls, as in the Lal Darwaza Masjid at Jaunpur"!! Further, he charged, the pillar bases were "easy to assemble" and brickbats that lay scattered had "been re-arranged by the ASI excavators to provide evidence for 'pillar bases'"!!!

After the Report had been submitted, Professor Habib condemned it as "an unprofessional document, full of gross omissions, one-sided presentations of evidence, clear falsifications and motivated inferences." Its only aim, he alleged, seemed to be to ignore and twist evidence to support the fiction of the Sangh Parivar about the earlier existence of a temple (Noorani I 2003: 163).

Similar insinuations were made by Suraj Bhan. When asked what, in his view, lay beneath Babri Masjid, he proclaimed, "...it was not a temple." It could be a mosque of the Sultanate period (*Frontline* 26 September 2003; page 3928 para 3823; pages 3955-56 para 3829; page 3821 para 3799).

It is pertinent to recall that with the exception of Suraj Bhan, none of the pro-Babri archaeologists had any experience of field archaeology. R.C. Thakran professed in Court that he was "just a table archaeologist ..." (pages 3853-56 para 3800). D. Mandal admitted that he had "acquired knowledge of archaeology." He had never obtained "any degree or diploma in archaeology" (page 3654 para 3628). Shereen Ratnagar also accepted that "in India I have not done any digging and excavation on my own" (page 4033 para 3852). Even Suraj Bhan acknowledged that he had conducted excavations only prior to writing his Ph. D thesis, which had not been published (pages 3624-27 para 3613).

Despite their obvious limitations, pro-Babri archaeologists were quick to disparage the work of the ASI. Of the 34 objections filed between 14th April 2003 and 26th July 2003, as many as 32 were on behalf of the Babri parties (page 3740 para 3676).

The Court felt constrained to comment on their deliberate attempts at misinformation (page 3774 para 3712; page 3767 para 3702). The Court observed that when structures underneath began to appear, the complainants, in consultation with "their alleged experts," started "preparing a kind of anticipatory ground to assail the ASI people, their proceedings and report" (pages 3775-76 para 3717).

Professor Habib, on his part, criticized the ASI for never having thought of comparing the circular shrine "with circular walls and buildings of Muslim construction" (Noorani I 2003: 167-68). Suraj Bhan, however, admitted,

> ... it was the in situ photograph of the circular shrine ... It is correct to say that a drain is visible in north orientation of plate no. 60. This construction is prior to the Islamic period (page 3823).

R.C. Thakran also conceded,

> A slender drain is visible to me on the north side in the picture below figure 17 on page 70A of the ASI report Volume I. It is correct to say that as per this figure 70, this drain is going northwards. It is also correct to say that the Buddhist stupas do not have such north-bound drains (page 3857)... The circular structure and the wall are possibly of the Gupta period (page 3861).

The Court described as "unthinkable" attempts to identify the shrine as a Muslim tomb. The circular structure displayed all the features of an independent miniature Shiva shrine of the ninth-tenth century (pages 4239-41 paras 3935-38; pages 4240-41 para 3939). The structure was too small to be a tomb, being only 4.4 ft. square from inside. It could neither accommodate a grave, nor a *qiblah-mihrab* on its western wall, the *qiblah* being an essential part of tomb-structures during the Sultanate period (page 4241 para 3940-41). Most important, a *pranala* was never found in tombs, but was an essential feature of Shiva temples (page 4241 para 3942). The refusal of pro-Babri groups to take cognizance of these facts, led the Court to observe the 'ostrich attitude' of the plaintiff (page 4241 para 3943).

The circular shrine recovered by the ASI was a subsidiary shrine, where the devotees offered *abhishek* from outside. Several examples have been cited for comparing the style of the shrine (Mani, *Puratattva* Number 33, 2002-2003: 104-13).

LIME, MORTAR, *SURKHI*

Professor Habib alleged that lime, mortar, and *surkhi*, "the recognized marks of Muslim construction," were present in practically all the excavated walls at Ayodhya. According to him, the find of lime mortar and surkhi down to the lowest layers of brickwork at the Rama Chabutara "sets at rest speculation about any pre-Muslim construction under it." The ASI had provided no examples of the use of *surkhi* in Gahadavala times, when the temple was allegedly constructed (Noorani I 2003: 144, 166).

However, lime mortar, lime plaster, and *surkhi* had been in use in India well before the advent of Muslims. Lime and gypsum had been discovered from the Indus Valley Civilization (page 4315). Jaya Menon admitted in Court,

> I agree ... that gypsum mortar/plaster was used in the Harappan period ... gypsum was used as mortar in the Kalibangan period also... Lime mortar was definitely used from Neolithic period (page 3853).

Surkhi was in use from early Kushan times. Suraj Bhan also conceded,

> It is correct to say that lime mortar was found to have been used in the 3rd century AD during the Kushan period in Takshshila and Pakistan, but its use was very limited (pages 3834-35).

Examples of the use of *surkhi* were available from Vikramshila (district Bhagalpur), where patches of thick plaster made of strong *surkhi* and lime were noticed on the walls and pillar bases (*Indian Archaeology 1971-72 — A Review*: 4). Lime plastered floors were found at the Gollathagudi temple in District Mahbubnagar, Andhra Pradesh, built in the twelfth century, and excavated by Muhammad Waheed Khan in 1970 (*Indian Archaeology 1971-72 – A Review*: 3). The use of *surkhi* in the Gahadavala period could also be verified at the Dharmachakrajin Vihara in Sarnath, constructed by the wife of Govindachandra.

Earlier, Professor R.S. Sharma had himself stated that *surkhi* was used as mortar and binding material in the early Christian era, when urbanism reached a high point in Northern and Western India. At Mathura and Ganwaria in Basti district in north-eastern U.P., the flooring was made of brick concrete mixed with lime. This indicated "the use of *surkhi*" (Sharma 1983: 181-82).

MIHRAB, NICHE, *QANATI* MOSQUE, IDGAH

The discovery of three recessed niches in Wall 16 (*Ayodhya: 2002-03*, Vol. I: ASI 2003: 68), another element of a temple, was also rejected by the pro-Babri group. According to Professor Habib the niches were additional proof of an earlier mosque below Babri Masjid. He said the ASI had made the base of an arched recess (*mihrab*) and an arched niche (*taq*) into features of the alleged temple (Noorani I 2003: 144). The position of the niches and recesses showed that they belonged to a *qanati* mosque/ idgah or some other Muslim structure. Temple niches would have to be on the outer, not inner wall, he maintained.

But a *qanati* mosque (a 'curtain' mosque, so-called after a *qanat*, curtain) is a wall mosque, and does not have pillars or a prayer hall. It is a mere wall with 5, 7, or 11 arches. A single arch cannot make a *qanati* mosque. A *qiblah-mihrab*, i.e. an arch in the centre of the western wall indicating the direction of Mecca, is an arch roofed by a half-cup shaped vault, both of which have great lateral thrust. That is why stone nook-shafts are normally used on the corners of such a mihrab. These were not found on the corners of the niche at Ayodhya. Structurally there was no arch or vault. As the Report stated, there was just a single rectangular niche.

Further, the floor-level of the niche was three courses higher than the floor level of the room in which it opened, a clear indication that it was made as an *'alaya'* for placement of an image or some similar purpose. The *mihrab* and the prayer hall of a mosque are always on the same level. A *mihrab* is never built on a higher level, as a niche, for placing things. An idgah has no niche; it is a plain, straight wall.

Moreover, as only the lower part of the niche had survived, it could not be said with certainty that it had an arched shape at the top. Also, niches could be inside and outside a temple; in Kashmir from the eighth century onwards, they were inside (Mitra 1993). R. Nath, retired Professor and Head of the Department of History and Indian Culture, at the University of Rajasthan, corroborated that no *taq* had been found in the excavations (page 4321-22).

Since this was the first time it was being pleaded that a *qanati* mosque or idgah lay below Babri Masjid, the Court expressed surprise at this possibility. On cross examination, Suraj Bhan disclosed that he had formed this opinion before the ASI had submitted its Report. He said this had been done to counter the "propaganda" that the remains of a temple had been found. He deposed,

> Consequent to submission of ASI's report in the matter and the claim that remains of temple were found at the disputed site, I and Prof. Habib had given this statement that remains of an old mosque or Eidgah had been found beneath the disputed site and not of any temple. If this propaganda that remains of temple were found at the disputed site, had not taken place, there would have been no occasion for me and Prof. Irfan Habib to give the above statement (pages 4295-96 para 3982; pages 3947-48 para 3826).

The Court was "surprised" that in their zeal to help the parties in whose favour they were appearing, these witnesses "wrote totally a new story" (pages 4298-99 para 3986). The Court observed that in D. Mandal's book, *Ayodhya: Archaeology after Demolition. A Critique of the 'New' and 'Fresh' Discoveries*, published in 1993, "there is not even a whisper" that a structure like an idgah or *qanati* mosque could possibly be underneath Babri Masjid (page 3709 para 3651).

The Court took cognizance of the shifting stance of the pro-Babri archaeologists. Initially they said that the disputed structure (DS) was constructed on a spot that was neither a place of worship, nor the site of any previous Hindu religious structure, nor was there any evidence to associate it with the birthplace of Lord Rama. However, as the excavations progressed, "a marked change in the approach of the plaintiffs became evident." Some archaeologists appearing on behalf of the plaintiffs tried to "set up a new case," that there appeared to be an Islamic structure beneath the DS (pages 3869-70 para 3809).

GLAZED TILES AND GLAZED WARE

The ASI reported the recovery of glazed tiles mainly from the debris and dump of the disputed structure (DS) and also from Period VIII and IX levels. It stated,

> Although use of glazed tiles in India can be traced back to the early centuries of Christian era when the Kushans introduced them, the tiles under study at present, most probably belong to the original construction of the disputed structure (*Ayodhya: 2002-03*, Vol.1 ASI 2003: 163).

The technique of glazing was known in China, and in 1942, H. Waddington had expressed the view that glazing came to India from China during the Kushan period. He said there were references to Chinese travellers visiting Mathura at that time and it was quite likely that Chinese pilgrims brought glazed ware in the form of votive stupas. A. Ghosh, in *An Encyclopedia of Indian Archaeology,* Vol. I, had reported the discovery of "a heavy turquoise blue glaze" at Chaubara and Maholi mounds, near Mathura, and several other sites in the vicinity, which dated to the Kushan period (Sharma 2011: 111-13).

Professor Irfan Habib was, however, categorical that glazed ware was definitive proof that negated the existence of a temple. Such ware, often called "Muslim" glazed ware, was never used in temples (Noorani I 2003: 164). D. Mandal made the same point in Court, "... (Period 4) here we begin to find glazed ware associated with the Muslim culture from the Sultanate period ..." (page 3973 para 3830).

Contrary to these assertions, glazed tiles had been found in the Buddhist structure at Shahji Dheri. Huien Tsang had noted the use of coloured tiles in several places in north India (page 4287 para 3976).

The Court observed that the excavations had made it "very clear" that the disputed structure was not raised on vacant land. The land in question had been in frequent use for several centuries continuously, and was "a place connected with religious purposes." The only thing to be determined was "whether it could be a temple or not." The Muslim parties had never before said that an Islamic religious structure existed at the place before the construction of Babri Masjid; or that a religious structure other than Hindu had existed (pages 4287-88 para 3977).

RAM CHABUTARA

The ASI excavations revealed that the Ram Chabutara had not less than five different structural phases of construction. Its original use was unclear; it could well have been a water tank. In its final form at the time of its last usage, it looked like a small platform. However, it was found to be a fairly large structure when its core was exposed, nearly 22 m in east-west and about 14 m in north-south orientation. The earliest form of the Ram Chabutara appeared to match the description of the Jesuit priest, Joseph Tieffenthaler (who visited the site between AD 1766 and 1771). He described it as a square box or *vedi* (elevated 5 inches above the ground level and covered with limestone), which was circumambulated thrice and saluted by people, who prostrated themselves on the ground (*Ayodhya: 2002-03*, Vol. I: ASI 2003: 49-51).

MASSIVE STRUCTURE

The ASI discovery of a "massive structure" below Babri Masjid, the remnants of which included a 50 m long wall (Wall 16) in the west and seventeen rows of pillar bases to its east, was also challenged by Left historians and archaeologists. They alleged that "a purely Muslim structure is being appropriated as a Hindu one" (pages 4202-13 para 3919; page 3868 para 3806; pages 4260-61 para 3959). Professor Habib called this "a regular part of the VHP kind of propagandist archaeology rather than a report from a body called the Archaeological Survey of India" (Noorani I 2003: 165-66).

The Court noted that the DS was shown resting over pillar base No. 29. Wall 6 (foundation wall of the southern chamber of the Masjid) was directly resting over two pillar bases, No. 34 and 35. Wall 7 (foundation wall of the southern chambers of the Masjid towards the east) was resting over three pillar bases (Nos. 29, 32, and 35). Wall 12 (northern wall of the northern chamber of the Masjid) rested over pillar base No. 22. The Court found the opinion of the pro-Babri archaeologists in respect of walls and floors "shaky and uncertain" (page 4229 paras 3927-28).

PILLAR BASES

Perhaps the most contentious section of the ASI Report pertained to the pillar bases. Professor Habib asserted that the pillar bases were one or more concrete stones resting on brick-bats, bonded with mud or just heaped up. Not a single pillar base, he said, had been found in association with any pillar or even a fragment of it. There were no marks on any concrete stones to show that any pillar had rested on them. Nor had the ASI attempted to answer why brickbats, and not bricks, were used at the base. The ASI had not provided any example of a medieval temple where pillars stood on such brickbats. Further, Professor Habib argued, the pillars were not in alignment. According to him, the pillar bases were deposits to fill up holes in the floors. Since such repairs were needed at various times all over the floors, the brickbat deposits were widely dispersed (Noorani I 2003: 166-67).

Both Jaya Menon and Supriya Verma accused the ASI of having created the pillar bases (pages 4138-46 para 3886; pages 4146-55 para 3887; pages 4155-62 para 3888).

The accusation stunned the Court, which noted that the excavations had been conducted in the presence of the plaintiffs, their experts, nominees and advocates, and also supervised by Court appointed observers. Under these circumstances, it could not accept that "the excavation has not been done faithfully and correctly" (pages 3793-94 para 3755; page 3792 para 3754). The Court stated that two members of the Higher Judicial Service appointed by the Court were present at the site as Observers. Also, both Suraj Bhan and D. Mandal had admitted that "in June 2003 they had no idea or information that any structure was manipulated by the members of the Archaeological Team of ASI" (pages 4129-30 para 3880).

The Court regarded it "really unfortunate" that neither Jaya Menon nor Supriya Verma could corroborate their complaints during cross examination. It stated,

> As admitted by these two witnesses, they were partisan and interested, yet it was expected from the renowned Experts that they shall tender opinion objectively but here we found it lacking.

The Court, for instance, pointed out that in Trench F9, the GPR Survey had indicated an anomaly at the depth of 0.5 m and the ASI had found a pillar base at that depth. Supriya Verma had not gone through the GPR report but dismissed the ASI find, "I could say that they were created pillar bases" (page 3787 para 3746; pages 3777-87 paras 3722-45).

The Court noted that in the two major complaints, dated 21st May 2003 and 7th June 2003, when excavations were on, the allegations on pillar bases were mainly made in those very trenches where the GPR Survey had already detected anomalies. It observed that the complainants "were already to some extent aware of likelihood of finding pillar bases in those trenches." Trenches N. F1, F6, F8, F9, G1, G2, G5, G8, G9, H1, ZG1 and ZH1 were in that category. It stated,

> ...the mind of two experts instead of working for the assistance of the Court in finding a truth, tried to create a background alibi so that later on the same may be utilized to attack the very findings (page 4177 para 3900).

The Court noted that the basic finding of the ASI report was, "There existed a structure and using part thereof either in the form of foundation or material thereof DS was created" (pages 4298-99 para 3986). The ASI had given "sufficient indication" that the DS did not have its foundations but was raised on existing walls. The floor of the DS was just over the floor of the earlier building. The existence of several pillar bases showed the existence of an earlier "sufficiently bigger structure, if not bigger than the disputed structure then not lesser than that also" (pages 4306-07 para 3990).

However, in an article, "Was There a Temple under the Babri Masjid? Reading the Archaeological 'Evidence'" (*Economic & Political Weekly* 11 December 2010: 61-72), Supriya Varma and Jaya Menon reiterated that the ASI had "created 50 'pillar bases' as further evidence for the temple." They asserted that the creation of "pillar bases" was "observed first-hand on several occasions in different trenches" (*Economic & Political Weekly* 11 December 2010: 65-66).

FIGURINES, STONE ARCHITECTURAL FRAGMENTS

In the course of excavations, the ASI found many figurines and stone architectural fragments like *amalaka*, pillar with *ghata-pallava* base with dwarf beings as weight-bearers, *kirtimukhas*, and divine couple as well as miscellaneous objects which further confirmed the non-Muslim nature of the structure beneath the Masjid (*Ayodhya: 2002-03*, Vol. I ASI 2003: 121-203). The pro-Babri archaeologists procrastinated here as well (page 3868; pages 4257-58 para 3957; pages 4260-61 para 3959; page 4256 para 3956; page 4259 para 3959).

The Court noted that none of the eight archaeologists of the Muslim parties claimed to be experts in the branch of archaeology that involved identification of excavated material like human or animal figurines etc. It stated,

> We have seen photographs of many of such artifacts and find and in generality there is no such inherent lacuna or perversity in the observations of ASI ... It is not in dispute that no Islamic religious artifacts have been found during excavation while artifacts relating to Hindu religious nature were in abundance... (pages 4258-59 para 3958).

Subsequently in the *Economic & Political Weekly* article cited above, Supriya Varma and Jaya Menon stated that of the 445 architectural fragments listed in the ASI Report, only 40 came from stratified contexts and none was specific to a temple. The twelve specifically mentioned in the Report all came from the debris lying on the surface of the mound, not from excavations under the Babri Masjid and "could have been introduced from anywhere." The twelve pieces included a stone slab with a *srivatsa* motif which, they said, was associated with Jainism; a stone slab with a lotus design that could be a Buddhist or Jain symbol; and a stone slab with a lozenge drawing that probably belonged to the Masjid itself (*Economic & Political Weekly* 11 December 2010: 64).

ANIMAL BONES

The pro-Babri archaeologists charged the ASI of ignoring animal bones that had been found at practically all levels. They also charged the ASI of not having kept records of the bones found at site (pages 4261-65 para 3960). Jaya Menon (pages 4267-69 para 3963).

The Court noted that during excavations animal bones were recovered from the fills of different periods. These fills were evidently brought from neighbouring areas to level the ground from time to time. It was natural that fills brought from habitational deposits contained animal bones. Their examination, therefore, would throw light only on the area of their origin. It had no bearing on the nature of the layers of the excavated site (page 4275 para 3968).

Further, the Court noted that it was not the case that bones in such abundance could have been found in an Islamic religious place like a mosque or idgah. Islamic scriptures were unambiguous that places of worship could not be used for residential purposes or for eating, sleeping etc. That being so, the existence of bones could have been of some importance if some other material had been found to suggest a residential place or if there had been a dispute about the nature of habitation. However, from the evidence and submission of Experts it was clear that they were aware that the structure below the Masjid was not a non-religious one (page 4276 para 3970).

INSCRIPTIONS

The ASI Report contained a brief note on three fragments of inscriptions found during excavations, one in Nagari and two in Arabic. One of the Arabic inscriptions, in Naskh style of the sixteenth century, comprised a verse from the Quran. The second Arabic inscription, also in the early sixteenth century style, contained the word Allah (*Ayodhya: 2002-03*, Vol. I: ASI 2003: 204-06).

The five letter inscription in Nagari was dated by ASI to the eleventh century AD. The dating, too, was questioned by the pro-Babri archaeologists, who held it could be in the range from seventh to twelfth centuries. They argued that it could be a Pala record of Buddhist provenance, "a piece of evidence negativing the presence of a Hindu temple" (page 4289).

Interestingly, Justice S.U. Khan also expressed disagreement with the ASI Report. In his view, it was abundantly clear that no temple was demolished for constructing the mosque. Further, until the mosque was raised, the disputed premises "was neither treated nor believed to be the birth-place nothing but the birth-place and the whole birth-place of Lord Rama." Justice Khan found it

> inconceivable that Babar (or Aurangzeb) should have first made or got made thorough research to ascertain the exact birth-place of Lord Rama, which was not known to anyone for centuries and then got constructed the mosque on the said site (Justice S.U. Khan pages 240-46).

Justice S.U. Khan held that till the mosque was built, Hindus believed that

> somewhere in a very large area of which premises in dispute is a very small part, birthplace of Lord Rama is situated. However, the belief did not relate to any specified small area within that bigger area specifically the premises in dispute. (It was some time after the construction of the mosque that the Hindus started identifying the premises in dispute) as exact birth place of Lord Rama or a place wherein exact birth place was situated ...

Justice Khan endorsed the view that

> there were also ruins of some Buddhist religious place on and around the land on which the mosque was constructed and some material thereof was used in the construction of mosque (Justice S.U. Khan pages 240-46).

12

No Mention of Babri Masjid in the Revenue Records

LAND REVENUE RECORDS

Professor B.R. Grover examined the revenue records relating to village Ram Kot, Haveli Awadh, available at the District Record Office (Mahafaz Khana/ Tehsil Office/ Nazul Office) at Faizabad, to determine the ownership of the Janmasthan/ Babri Masjid. The records comprised various categories of revenue documents like survey, *bandobast* (settlement), *kishtwar khasra, abadi, khewats, khasra khataunis* and maps etc., from AD 1861 to 1990-91. They revealed that from the time of the first Regular Settlement in 1861, the land was shown as Nazul (Government) and this had not been disputed or challenged by anyone.

The first Regular Settlement Report of Kot Ram Chandra, appended by two maps, was the most comprehensive document relating to the Janmasthan complex comprising Rama Janmabhumi. It was prepared after an on the spot survey and measurement of the *khasras* relating to *kishtwar* and *abadi*, and, in accordance with the erstwhile Nawabi and Mughal practice, was duly attested in every respect by the local *zamindars/*

pattidars of various *mahal* units, the local revenue officials and witnesses etc. The Report was also based on the previous summary settlements of 1858-60, and depicted the exact position of Janmasthan/Babri Masjid and the neighbouring plots as inherited from the Nawabi period. In the revenue documents, the superior ownership of the land had been declared in the name of Sarkar Bahadur Nazul (Government) and the Mahants had been declared the under-proprietors (*malikan-i-matahit*) of the entire Janmasthan complex.

The Settlement Report of 1893 clearly mentioned the sub-plot on which the Masjid was situated as Sita Ki Rasoi. The subsequent Settlement Reports of 1936-37 and 1989-90 maintained the same position. There was no record of the Babri Masjid in the documents preserved by the Revenue Department of the Government at the Collectorate and Tehsil at Faizabad (Grover 1994: 343-49).

In its judgement, the Allahabad High Court held that this document was an acknowledgement that the entire Mauja had been entered as Nazul. The Muslim parties argued in Court that the entry as Nazul in British records was wrongly made. However, it was indisputable that even in the first settlement of 1861, the land was shown as Nazul and that status had never been questioned (page 2313 para 2328; pages 5001-07 paras 4427-33).

UNAUTHORIZED INTERPOLATIONS IN THE REVENUE RECORDS

Professor Grover detected several interpolations/additions in the *khasra kishtwar* folios in the original Settlement Report of AD 1861, available at the District Record Office, Faizabad.

In column No. 2, to the original record of *'abadi Janmasthan,'* the words *'and Juma Masjid'* had been added, so as to read *'abadi Janmasthan and Juma Masjid.'*

In column No. 3 to the words *'taraf nazul,' 'and muafi'* had been inserted.

In column No. 4 to the words *'Sarkar Bahadur'* had been added *'wa Azhar Hussain'*. The ink, the thickness of the letters, the handwriting, undoubtedly indicated additions (Grover 2015: 119-21).

Copies of the same documents prepared the same year available at the Tehsil Office clearly proved the changes, done perhaps during the preceding few decades of the controversy. This was also confirmed by the fact that the *khasra kishtwar* records of the second Revenue Settlement of the year 1301 *Fasli* (AD 1893) did not carry the alterations or additions. These records still showed the area on which Babri Masjid had been constructed as Sita Ki Rasoi, forming a part of the Janmasthan complex (vide Khasra No. 163/5). There was no mention of any mosque, nor land assigned to it in *muafi* (Grover 2015: 87-88, 120-21, 234-35).

Most significantly, the map of the Hadbast of village Kot Ramachandra, Pargana Haveli, Tehsil and Zilla Faizabad, prepared in 1861 showed only the temple at the Janmasthan in a significant manner; Babri Masjid was not even indicated, even though the physical structure of the mosque existed on a part of the plot where only the Janmasthan temple was shown.

In another related map, the Masjid had been put in a most insignificant symbol. The revised *khasra* records of 1344-45 *Fasli* (1937-38) reiterated the same position as recorded in the earlier settlements, except that in one of the plots, both Masjid and Chabutara, indicating the temple at Janmasthan, had been recorded. The mosque had been shown in *waqf* under the column 'Name of the Present Possessor' (*Nam Hal Qabiz*). Mahant Raghu Nath Das had been declared under-proprietor of the entire plot. Such a position occurred for the first time in the *khasra* records, which had been regularly prepared since 1858-59 and 1861. Apparently the change was made by the British Government in the aftermath of the 1934 riots. However, this was not further reflected in other related revenue documents available since 1937-38 (Grover 2015: 235).

NO WAQF FOR BABRI MASJID

Equally conclusive, the revenue documents from 1858-61 to 1991 revealed that no Waqf land had ever been associated with Babri Masjid (Grover 2015: 171-84). As per the UP Muslim Waqfs Act of 1936, a survey of Waqf property in the state was conducted by the Commissioner of Waqfs. The UP Government forwarded his Report, along with the list of Shia Waqfs to the Shia Central Board of Waqfs, and of the Sunni Waqfs to the Sunni Central Board of Waqfs. Each Waqf Board was required to publish the Report with its list in the Official Gazette, under subsection (1) of Section 5. The Report and the lists were accordingly published in the UP Gazette, dated 26th February 1944. There was no mention any Waqf for Babri Masjid. The absence of any mention of Waqf was regarded a "fatal flaw" in the case of the pro-Babri parties by the Allahabad High Court.

13

The Allahabad High Court Judgement on the Ramjanmabhumi/ Babri Masjid Case

On 30th September 2010, the Allahabad High Court delivered its verdict on the five suits pending before it. The Court decreed that the area covered by the central dome of the disputed structure "being the deity of Bhagwan Ram Janmasthan and the birthplace of Lord Rama as per faith and belief of the Hindus," belonged to the plaintiffs (Bhagwan Sri Ram Lalla Virajman and others; Suit 5). The area within the inner courtyard belonged to Hindus and Muslims as the two communities had used it for centuries. The area covered by the structures Rama Chabutara, Sita ki Rasoi, and Bhandar in the outer courtyard belonged to the Nirmohi Akhara. The open area within the outer courtyard, except that mentioned above, would be shared between the Nirmohi Akhara and plaintiffs (Suit 5) as it had been used by the Hindus to worship at both places. The share of the Muslims would not be less than one-third of the total area of the premises, and if necessary, they could be given some area of the outer courtyard. The land the Government had acquired in 1993 should be provided to the parties "in such a manner so that all the three parties may utilize the area to which they are entitled to, by having separate entry for egress and ingress of the people without disturbing each others rights" (pages 5079-81 para 4566; Justice S.U. Khan pages 284-85).

The Court clarified that it was the belief of the Hindus that the birthplace of Lord Rama was confined to the area under the central dome. In Jamshedji Cursetjee Tarachand vs. Soonabai, the Bombay High Court had said, "If this is the belief of the community ... a secular judge is bound to accept that belief – it is not for him to sit in judgement of that belief" (pages 4996-97 para 4412, 4414). The Allahabad High Court observed,

> once such belief gets concentrated to a particular point ...it partakes the nature of an essential part of religion particularly when it relates to a matter which is of peculiar significance to a religion. It, therefore, stands on a different footing. Such an essential part of religion is constitutionally protected under Article 25 (pages 4997-98 para 4415).

The Allahabad High Court was satisfied that the place of birth "as believed and worshipped by Hindus" was the area under the central dome (page 4999 para 4418).

Further, in the outer premises existed the Ram Chabutara, Sita ki Rasoi, and Bhandar, which had been confirmed by two maps of the years 1885 and 1950. These structures were demolished on 6th December 1992. They had been possessed and managed by the Nirmohi Akhara, and this had not been refuted by anyone (page 5000 para 4421; pages 5045-46 paras 4492-93).

The Court also held that the disputed structure was constructed as a mosque and treated as a mosque by Hindus and Muslims. But despite that, Hindus continuously entered and worshipped the place "since, according to their belief, it was the place of birth of Lord Rama and therefore, could not have been desecrated so as to extinguish in any manner ..." The property in dispute had a dual character; it was the birthplace of Lord Rama and a Swyambhu deity, which would continue so long as the place continued. Simultaneously Muslims also offered their worship at the same site (pages 5000-01 paras 4423-24; pages 5035-36 para 4488; page 5046 para 4494).

However, it had not been proved that namaaz had been offered at the building since 1528. The Court expressed the view that namaaz was offered intermittently between 1860 and 16th December 1949. Jawed Husain, who was said to be the Mutawalli of Babri Masjid, and Abdul Gaffar, who claimed to be Imam, at no point took steps to protect the building; "not even a complaint was filed by anyone of them." It appeared to the Court that Jawed Husain was not properly appointed Mutawalli; he simply enjoyed the grant of the villages of Sholapur and Bhuraipur and was called "*Numberdar*" thereof. However, in the absence of any other claimant, he could be treated as *de facto* Mutawalli. The management being the responsibility of a Mutawalli, the possession of waqf could also be claimed by him, since as a worshipper he was not entitled to possession of waqf property. No relief could be allowed to plaintiffs (Suit 4), who had come before the Court "in the capacity of worshippers and not the person who can claim possession of waqf, i.e., a Mutawalli" (pages 5048-51 para 4500-05).

The Court noted that a place of "non-Islamic character" existed at the site before the construction of the disputed structure. The accounts of William Finch and Joseph Tieffenthaler attested to continuous Hindu worship there. The "cumulative effect" of all the facts presented in Court left no doubt that even before the construction of the disputed structure, Hindus used to worship at the place they believed to be the birthplace of Rama (pages 5058-59 para 4521). The area under the central dome was a place of special significance for the Hindus and had to be treated in a manner "where the very right of worship of Hindus of place of birth of Lord

Rama is not extinguished or otherwise interfered with" (pages 5073-74 para 4559). So the continuity of title and possession of the deities remains unhindered.

The day after the judgement was delivered, a statement was released by Sahmat, signed, among others, by Professors Romila Thapar, D.N. Jha, Shireen Moosvi, Irfan Habib, D. Mandal, Supriya Verma, Jaya Menon, and Sita Ram Roy. It criticized the Court for accepting the claim that Hindus had since times immemorial believed that the Babri Masjid marked the site of Rama's birthplace and converting that into an argument for deciding property entitlement. By its judgement the Court had provided legitimacy "to violence and muscle power," and acknowledged the demolition of the Babri Masjid in 1992 "as an act whose consequences are to be accepted, by transferring the main parts of the mosque to those clamouring for a temple to be built" (Sahmat 2010a: 5-6).

Continuing the campaign, in an article in *The Hindu* on 2nd October 2010, Professor Romila Thapar described the verdict as "a political judgement" and a "response to an appeal by Hindu faith and belief." By endorsing one point of view, the Court had created a precedent that land could be claimed by declaring it the birthplace "of a divine or semi-divine being worshipped by a group that defines itself as a community." The High Court decision had "annulled respect for history and seeks to replace history with religious faith." Professor Thapar regretted that in the summary of the verdict there was no mention of the "act of wanton destruction" of Babri Masjid, which was "part of our cultural heritage."

Professor Irfan Habib in turn, attacked the "astonishingly one-sided" nature of the decision, which was "an absolute legitimation" of the demolition of Babri Masjid. The judges had treated the issue of Hindu faith in the exact birth-place of Lord Rama as "the main decisive point." They had "lamentably failed to make what should be an elementary distinction between faith and propaganda." The conferment of juridical entity on "a supernatural power," Professor Habib argued, was inconsistent with the country's secular Constitution. It was vital for the Supreme Court to ensure that all courts below it did their duty to the People of India (*People's Democracy* 17th October 2010).

On what grounds can the Apex Court legitimately be expected to overturn this judgement? Rama has been linked with this land from early on. The antiquity of the Rama *Katha* has been traced as far back as sixth-fifth century BCE, when ancient ballads (*akhyanas*) transmitted Rama's story orally. Valmiki's *Ramayana* itself has been dated to the fourth-third century BCE. By the fourth-fifth century CE, the evolution of Rama from epic hero to incarnation of Vishnu to Supreme Reality had been more or less completed. By the twelfth century CE temples dedicated exclusively to Rama had begun to be built, and texts for the proper worship of the Lord composed. Over the centuries, Rama's story has been retold in many vernaculars of the country; there have been over three hundred retellings according to one count. Rama is the exemplar of moral values for Hindu society and epitomises its aspirations of *artha, kama,* and above all, *dharma*.

No evidence whatsoever has been proffered of continued Muslim occupation of Babri Masjid, while the uninterrupted presence of Hindu devotees has been attested by several sources. Babri Masjid finds no mention in the revenue records of the Nawabi and British periods, nor was any Waqf ever created for its upkeep. No Muslim filed an FIR or complained of dispossession or obstruction in his alleged use of the Masjid when the image of Sri Rama was placed under the central dome on 23rd December 1949. From that day worship at the site has continued unhindered.

The Sunni Central Waqf Board entered litigation on 18th December 1961, just five days before the twelfth anniversary of the placement of the image in the Masjid, on which date any claim would have become time-barred. The Board did not file a suit for possession; instead it sought a declaration on the status of the property.

The excavations of the ASI have revealed uninterrupted occupation of the site since the 13th century BCE. They have also exposed remnants of the temple on which Babri Masjid was erected.

So why has the matter dragged on for so long? Can a handful of historians be held accountable for stalling resolution of what is essentially a settled matter? Their voluble assertions on Babri Masjid have all been found to be erroneous; yet there has been no public retraction. Are they liable for vitiating social harmony over this issue? If the nation has to move on, honest answers must be found to these questions.

For the moment, it's over to the Supreme Court.

Select Bibliography

NATIONAL ARCHIVES OF INDIA

Home Political Branch B April 1913, Nos. 109-114
Home Political Branch B, April 1913, Nos. 109-114
Home Department Political F. No. 5/2/1934 Poll
Foreign Department Political 28 December 1855, No. 351-358 & KW
Foreign Department Political 28 December 1855, No.450 & KW

ARCHAEOLOGICAL SOURCES

Ayodhya: 2002-03. Vol. I: Archaeological Survey of India, 2003.

Cunningham, Alexander. 1871. *Four Reports Made During the Years 1862-63-64-65*, Vol. I, Archaeological Survey of India, reprinted, 2000.

Fuhrer, A. 1889. *The Sharqi Architecture of Jaunpur, with Notes on Zafarabad, Sahet-Mahet and Other Places in the North-Western Provinces and Oudh*, Archeological Survey of India.

——. 1891. *The Monumental Antiquities and Inscriptions in the North-Western Provinces and Audh*, Vol. II, Archeological Survey of India.

Indian Archaeology 1971-72 – A Review, Archeological Survey of India, 1975.

Indian Archaeology 1976-77 – A Review, Archaeological Survey of India, 1980.
Memoirs of the Archaeological Survey of India, No. 70, Archaeological Survey of India, 1999.

EPIGRAPHICAL SOURCES

Corpus Inscriptionum Indicarum
Epigraphia Indica
The Indian Antiquary

JOURNALS AND MAGAZINES

Economic and Political Weekly
Frontline
Muslim India
New Age
People's Democracy
Puratattva
Swarajya

NEWSPAPERS

The Hindu
The Hindustan Times
The Indian Express
The Statesman
The Times of India

JUDICIAL VERDICTS

Allahabad High Court Judgement of 30th September 2010.

FOREIGN ACCOUNTS

de Laet. 1928. *The Empire of the Great Mogul: De Laet's Description of India and Fragment of Indian History*, J.S. Hoyland (translated) and annotated by S.N. Banerjee, reprinted, 1974, Munshiram Manoharlal.
Foster, William. 1921. Ed. *Early Travels in India 1583-1619*, reprinted, 1999, Low Price Publications.
Herbert, Thomas. 1638. *Some Years Travels into Divers Parts of Asia and Afrique*, London.

Tieffenthaler, Joseph. 1786. *Description Historique Et Geographique De L'Inde*, published in French by M. Jean Bernoulli, A. Berlin.

BRITISH ACCOUNTS, GAZETTEERS

Balfour, Edward. 1858. *Encyclopaedia of India and of Eastern and Southern Asia*, London B. Quaritch.

Benett, W.C. 1877-78. *Gazetteer of Oudh*, 3 vols., reprinted, 1993, Low Price Publications.

Carnegy, P. 1870. *Historical Sketches of Tahsil Fyzabad, Zilla Fyzabad*, Oudh Government Press.

Hamilton, Walter. 1828. *A Geographical, Statistical, and Historical Description of Hindostan and the Adjacent Countries*, Vol. I, reprinted, 1971, Oriental Publishers.

Martin, Robert Montgomery. 1838. *The History, Antiquities, Topography and Statistics of Eastern India*, reprinted, 1976, Cosmo Publications.

Mettell, A.F. 1880. *Report of the Settlement of the Land Revenue, Fyzabad District*, Allahabad.

Thornton, Edward. 1858. *A Gazetteer of the Territories under the Government of the East-India Company*, reprinted, 1993, Low Price Publications.

Nevill, H.R. 1905. *Fyzabad: A Gazetteer*, Government Press, Allahabad.

MUSLIM SOURCES

Abul Fazl Allami. 1891. *The Ain-i Akbari*, translated from the original Persian by Colonel H.S. Jarrett, second edition corrected and further annotated by Sir Jadunath Sarkar, Vol. II, 1949, reprinted, 1978, Oriental Books Reprint Corporation.

Babur-Nama. 1922. Edited by A.S. Beveridge, reprinted, 1970, Oriental Books Reprint Corporation.

Leyden, John. 1826. *Memoirs of Zehir-ed-din Muhammad Babur, Emperor of Hindustan*, translated by J. Leyden and William Erskine, Longman.

Narain, Harsh. 1993. *The Ayodhya Temple-Mosque Dispute. Focus on Muslim Sources*, Penman Publishers.

Sachau, Edward C. 1888. ed., *Al-Biruni's India*, reprinted, 1989, Atlantic Publishers and Distributors.

Tuzuk-i-Jahangiri or Memoirs of Jahangir. 1914. Translated by Alexander Rogers, edited by Henry Beveridge, reprinted, 1968, Munshiram Manoharlal.

IMPERIAL *FARMANS*

Commissariat, M.S. 1940. "Imperial Mughal Farmans in Gujarat," in *Journal of the University of Bombay,* Vol. IX, Issue I.

Mukherjee, Tarapada and Irfan Habib. 1988. "Akbar and the Temples of Mathura and Its Environs," in *Proceedings of the Indian History Congress.*

BUDDHIST SOURCES

Cowell, E.B. 1901. Ed., *The Jataka or Stories of the Buddha's Former Births,* Translated from the Pali by various hands, Vol. IV, reprinted, 1990, Low Price Publications.

SECONDARY WORKS

Aggarwal, J.C. and N.K. Chowdhry. 1991. *Babri Masjid Controversy,* S. Chand & Company.

Agrawal, Jagannath. 1994. "Ayodhya from the Maurya to the Gupta Period," in Lallanji Gopal ed. *Ayodhya. History, Archaeology and Tradition,* All India Kashiraj Trust, Fort Ramnagar, Varanasi.

Altekar, A.S. 1947. *Benaras and Sarnath: Past and Present,* Banaras Hindu University.

Awasthi, A.B.L. 1983. *Studies in Skanda Purana,* Kailash Prakashan.

Asher, Catherine B. 1992. *Architecture of Mughal India,* The New Cambridge History of India, Cambridge University Press.

Bakker, Hans. 1986. *Ayodhya,* Egbert Forsten, Groningen.

——. 1991. "Ayodhya: A Hindu Jerusalem: An Investigation of 'Holy War' as a Religious Idea in the Light of Communal Unrest in India," in *Numen,* Vol. 38, Fasc 1, June.

Bhandarkar, R.G. 1913. *Vaisnavism, Saivism and Minor Religious Systems,* Bhandarkar Oriental Research Institute, reprinted, 1982.

Bhatnagar, G.D. 1968. *Awadh under Wajid Ali Shah,* Bharatiya Vidya Prakashan.

Bhatnagar, V.S. 1974. *Life and Times of Sawai Jai Singh. 1688-1743*, Impex India.

Bhatt, R.S. 2005. *Sawai Jai Singh*, translated by S.K. Jha, National Book Trust.

Brockington, John. 1984. *Righteous Rama. The Evolution of an Epic*, Oxford University Press.

——. 1998. *The Sanskrit Epics*, Brill.

Bulke, Camille. 1950. *Ramkatha: Utpatti aur Vikas*, Hindi Parisad Prakashan.

Burghart, Richard. 2005. "The Founding of the Ramanandi Sect," reprinted in David N. Lorenzen ed., *Religious Movements in South Asia 600-1800*, Oxford University Press.

Butler, John. 2012. *Sir Thomas Herbert's Travels in Africa, Persia and Asia the Great*, Arizona Centre for Medieval and Renaissance Studies.

Cole, J.R.I. 1988. *Roots of North Indian Shi'ism in Iran and Iraq. Religion and State in Awadh, 1772-1859*, University of California Press.

Davis, Richard. 2015. *Lives of Indian Images*, Motilal Banarsidass.

Desai, Kalpana S. 1973. *Iconography of Visnu*, Abhinav Publications.

Eck, Diana. 1983. *Banaras, City of Light*, Routledge and Kegan Paul.

Elst, Koenraad. 1990. *Ram Janmabhoomi* vs. *Babri Masjid*, Voice of India.

——. 1991. *Ayodhya and After*, Voice of India.

——. 2002. *Ayodhya. The Case against the Temple*, Voice of India.

——. 2003. *Ayodhya the Finale*, Voice of India.

Entwistle, A.W. 1987. *Braj: Centre of Krishna Pilgrimage*, Groningen.

Farquhar, J.N. 1967. *An Outline of the Religious Literature of India*, Munshiram Manoharlal.

Findly, Ellison B. 1987. "Jahangir's Vow of Non-violence," in *Journal of the American Oriental Society*, Vol. I, No. 2.

Fisher, Michael H. 1987. *A Clash of Cultures. Awadh, the British and the Mughals*, Manohar.

Ghurye, G.S. 1964. *Indian Sadhus*, Popular Prakashan, first published in 1953.

Godbole, Madhav. 1996. *Unfinished Innings. Recollections and Reflections of a Civil Servant*, Orient Longman.

Goldman, Robert P. 1984. *The Ramayana of Valmiki*, Vol. I, Introduction and Translation by Robert P. Goldman, Princeton University Press.

Gombrich, Richard. 1985. "The Vessantara Jataka, the Ramayana and the Dasaratha Jataka," in *Journal of the American Oriental Society, 105.*

Gopal, S. 1991. Ed. *Anatomy of a Confrontation. The Babri-Masjid-Ramjanmabhumi Issue*, Viking.

Goswamy, B.N. and J.S. Grewal 1967. *The Mughals and the Jogis of Jakhbar*, Indian Institute of Advanced Study.

Grover, B.R. 1994. "An Analysis of the Revenue Documents Relating to *Janmsthan* (Ram Janm Bhoomi) versus 'Babri Masjid' at Kot Ram Chandra, Awadh (Ayodhaya)," in Lallanji Gopal ed. *Ayodhya. History, Archaeology and Tradition*, All India Kashiraj Trust, Fort Ramnagar, Varanasi.

——. 2015. *Rama Janamabhoomi: Professor B.R. Grover's Analysis of Revenue Records and Historical Facts*, Originals.

Grover, B.R. and S.P. Gupta. 1991. "Janmasthan (Ram Janma Bhumi) versus 'Baburi Masjid'" in Vinay Chandra Mishra Ed. *Ram Janmabhoomi Babri Masjid. Historical Documents Legal Opinions and Judgements*, The Bar Council of India Trust, Universal Book Traders, verbatim of the Special issue of the Indian Bar Review, vol. XVIII (2).

Growse, F.S. 1882. *Mathura-A District Memoir*, reprinted, 1979, Asian Educational Services.

——. 1914 reprint. *The Ramayana of Tulsi Das*, Ram Narain Lal.

Habib, Irfan. 2007. "Medieval Ayodhya (Awadh), Down to the Mughal Occupation," paper presented at the 67th session of the Indian History Congress, *Proceedings of the Indian History Congress.*

History versus Casuistry. Evidence of the Ramjanmabhoomi Mandir presented by the Vishva Hindu Parishad to the Government of India in December-January 1990-91, Voice of India, July 1991.

Horstman, Monika. 1999a. *In Favour of Govinddevji. Historical Documents Relating to a Deity of Vrindaban and Eastern Rajasthan*, Manohar.

——. 2002. "The Ramanandis of Galta (Jaipur, Rajasthan)," in Lawrence A. Babb, Varsha Joshi and Michael W. Meister eds., *Multiple Histories. Culture and Society in the Study of Rajasthan*, Rawat Publications.

——. 2011. "Theology and Statecraft," in Rosalind O'Hanlon and David Washbrook eds., *Religious Cultures in Early Modern India*, Routledge.

Jacobi, Hermann. 1893. *Das Ramayana*, translated from the German by S.N. Ghosal, Oriental Institute, Baroda, 1960.

Jain, J.C. 1994. "Ayodhya in Jain Tradition," in Lallanji Gopal ed. *Ayodhya. History, Archaeology and Tradition*, All India Kashiraj Trust, Fort Ramnagar, Varanasi.

Jain, Meenakshi. 2013. *Rama and Ayodhya*, Aryan Books International.

Jaiswal, Suvira. 2013. "Historical Evolution of the Rama Legend," in D.N. Jha ed., *Contesting Symbols and Stereotypes*, Aakar.

Jawaharlal Nehru University. 1989. *The Political Abuse of History: Babri Masjid-Ramjanmabhumi Dispute – An Analysis by Twenty-Five Historians*, The Centre for Historical Studies, Jawaharlal Nehru University.

John, Jose K. 1997. "The Mapping of Hindustan: A Forgotten Geographer of India, Joseph Tieffenthaler (1710-1785)," in *Proceedings of the Indian History Congress*, 58th Session.

Joshi, Esha B. 1960. *UP District Gazetteers – Faizabad*, Government of Uttar Pradesh.

Kane, P.V. 1990. *History of Dharmasastra*, Vol. I Part I, Bhandarkar Oriental Research Institute.

Khushwant Singh. 2015. *A History of the Sikhs, Vol. I: 1469-1839*, Oxford University Press, first published in 1963.

Krishnamurti, R. 1961. *Akbar: The Religious Aspect*, Maharaja Sayajirao University of Baroda.

Kulkarni, V.M. 1980. "Jain *Ramayanas* and Their Source," in V. Raghavan ed., *The Ramayana Tradition in Asia*, Sahitya Akademi.

Kunal, Kishore. 2016. *Ayodhya Revisited*, Ocean Books.

Lal, B.B. 1988. "Historicity of the *Mahabharata* and the *Ramayana*: What has Archaeology to Say in the Matter," paper presented at a seminar on *New Archaeology and India*, Indian Council for Historical Research, Delhi.

Lannoy, Richard. 1999. *Banaras Seen from Within*, Indica Books.

Law, B.C. 1976. Reprint. *Historical Geography of Ancient India*, Ess Ess Publications.

Llewellyn-Jones, Rosie. 2015. *The Last King in India*, Random House India

Madhura Vijaya: A Historical Kavya. 1924. By Ganga Devi, ed. H. Sastri and V.S. Sastri, The Sridhara Power Press.

Mandal, D. 1993. *Ayodhya: Archaeology after Demolition*, Orient Longman.

Mandal, D. and Shereen Ratnagar. 2007. *Archaeology after Excavation*, Tulika Books.

Mehrotra, S.R. 2006. "The *Ramayana* Tradition in Modern India," in D.P. Saklani ed., *Ramayana Tradition in Historical Perspective*, Pratibha Prakashan.

Mirashi, V.V. 1966. *Studies in Indology*, Vol. IV, Tara Publications.

Mitra, Debala. 1993. *Pandrethan, Avantipur and Martand*, Archaeological Survey of India.

Nath, R. 1993a. "Sawai Jaisingh had acquired Ramjanmasthan in 1717 A.D." in *Observer of Business and Politics*, 6.1.1993.

——. 1993b. "Jaisingh had acquired land at Mathura, Kashi too" in *Observer of Business and Politics*, 7.1.1993.

——. 2004. *Kaal-Darpan*, Parimal Publications.

Niyogi, Roma. 1959. *The History of the Gahadavala Dynasty*, Calcutta Oriental Book Agency.

Noorani, A.G. 2003. ed., *The Babri Masjid Question, 1528-2003: 'A Matter of National Honour,'* 2 vols. Tulika Books.

——. 2015. *Destruction of Babri Masjid. A National Dishonour*, Tulika Books.

Okita, Kiyokazu. 2014. *Hindu Theology in Early Modern South Asia*, Oxford University Press.

Peabody, Norbert. 1991. "In Whose Turban Does the Lord Reside?: The Objectification of Charisma and the Fetishism of Objects in the Hindu Kingdom of Kota," in *Comparative Studies in Society and History*, Vol. 33, Issue 4.

Pollock, Sheldon. 1993. "*Ramayana* and Political Imagination in India," in *The Journal of Asian Studies*, 52, No. 2, May.

——. 1994. "Deep Orientalism? Notes on Sanskrit and Power Beyond the Raj," in Carol A. Breckenridge and Peter van der Veer eds., *Orientalism and the Postcolonial Predicament*, Oxford University Press.

Prasad, Pushpa. 1990. *Sanskrit Inscriptions of Delhi Sultanate 1191-1526*, Oxford University Press.

——. 2004. "Three Recently Found Inscriptions at Ayodhya," in *Proceedings of the Indian History Congress*, 64th Session.

Ramjanmabhumi-Babri Masjid: A Historians' Report to the Nation. 1991, in A.G. Noorani ed., *The Babri Masjid Question, 1528-2003: 'A Matter of National Honour,'* Vol. I, Tulika Books.

Raychaudhuri, H.C. 1920. *Materials for the Study of the Early History of the Vaishnava Sect*, University of Calcutta.

Roy, Jahnawi. S. 1994. "A Note on Ayodhya Inscription", in Lallanji Gopal ed. *Ayodhya. History, Archaeology and Tradition*, All India Kashiraj Trust, Fort Ramnagar, Varanasi.

Roy, Sita Ram. 1996. "Ayodhya in Literature and Archaeology," in K.M. Shrimali ed., *Indian Archaeology Since Independence*, Association for the Study of History and Archaeology.

Sahmat. 2010a. *On the Ayodhya Judgement of the Allahabad High Court*, Sahmat.

——. 2010b. *History and the Judgement of the Allahabad High Court (Lucknow Bench) in the Ramjanmabhumi-Babri Masjid Case.*

Sardesai, G.S. 1958. *New History of the Marathas*, Vol. II, Phoenix Publications.

Sarkar, J.N. 1966. *Fall of the Mughal Empire*, Vol. II, M.C. Sarkar & Sons.

——. 1984. *A History of Jaipur c. 1503-1938*, Orient Longman.

Sen, S.N. 1962. "Joseph Tieffenthaler and His Geography of Hindustan," in *Journal of the Asiatic Society*, Vol. IV, Nos. 3 and 4.

Sharma, A.K. 2011. *Ayodhya Case. Archaeological Evidence*, B.R. Publishing Corporation.

Sharma, R.S. 1983. *Perspectives in Social and Economic History of Early India*, Munshiram Manoharlal.

——. 1990. *Communal History and Rama's Ayodhya*, People's Publishing House.

Sharma, Y.D., et al. 1992. *Ramjanma Bhumi: Ayodhya. New Archaeological Discoveries*, Historians' Forum.

Shrimali, K.M. 2003 "Archaeology of Ayodhya: From Imbroglio to Resolution" in A.G. Noorani ed., *The Babri Masjid Question, 1528-2003: 'A Matter of National Honour,'* Vol. I, Tulika Books.

Sinha, Surendra Nath. 1976. *The Mid-Gangetic Region in the Eighteenth Century (Some Observations of Joseph Tieffenthaler)*, Shanti Prakashan.

Subrahmanyam, Sanjay. 2004. *Explorations in Connected History. From the Tagus to the Ganges*, Oxford University Press.

Thapar, Romila. 1989. "The Ramayana Syndrome," in *Seminar* 353, January.

——. 1991. "A Historical Perspective on the Story of Rama," in S. Gopal ed., *Anatomy of a Confrontation. The Babri-Masjid-Ramjanmabhumi Issue*, Viking.

Truschke, Audrey. 2012. "Setting the record wrong: a Sanskrit vision of Mughal conquests," *South Asian History and Culture*, Vol. 3. No. 3.

——. 2015. "Dangerous Debates: Jain responses to theological challenges at the Mughal court," in *Modern Asian Studies*, Vol. 49, Issue 5.

Vaudeville, Charlotte. 2005. *Myths, Saints and Legends in Medieval India*, Oxford University Press.

Veer, Peter van der. 1989. *Gods on Earth*, Oxford University Press.

Index

23rd December 1949 75, 144

Abul Fazl Allami 1, 13
Agastya Samhita 86, 89
Akbar 1, 8-9, 37, 44
Al-Biruni 46
Ali, Athar 6, 92, 99
Ali, Maulvi Amir 57-58
Ali, Mir Rajib 60
Allahabad High Court 2, 9, 60, 62, 64-66, 69, 73-74, 82, 101, 105-06, 111, 137, 139-41
Archaeological Survey of India 5, 7, 94, 97-98, 116, 130
Asghar, Muhammad 59-62, 113
ASI Report 116, 120-21, 124, 128, 130, 132-35
Avadha vilasa 91
Ayodhya 1, 3-7, 9-12, 14-15, 17, 20, 30, 32-34, 43-45, 49-50, 52-54, 57-58, 70-76, 78-79, 81-83, 88, 90-98, 100-01, 104-10, 116-21, 125-28, 130, 133-34
Ayodhya Mahatmya 5, 90, 92-93, 100, 106

Babri Masjid 2-3, 5, 7, 12, 17, 48, 51-52, 59-62, 65-66, 71-73, 75, 78-79, 94-98, 100-101, 103, 105, 107, 109, 111, 113, 115-16, 119-23, 126-30, 132-33, 136-39, 142-45
Babri Masjid Action Committee (BMAC) 5
Babur 4, 11-16, 18, 29, 32, 50, 53, 67, 70, 91, 100, 113-14
Bahadur, Beni 44
Bahadur, Girdhar 43
Bakker, Hans 4, 89-92, 110
Balfour, Surgeon General Edward 30
Banaras 34, 41, 44, 49, 82, 86, 89, 94

Benett, W.C. 30
Beveridge, Annette S. 12
Bhan, Suraj 6, 92, 99, 122-25, 127, 131
Bhavartha Ramayana 87
Braj 34, 36-37, 39-40

Carnegy, Patrick 30, 43, 57
Chamier, Col. F.E.A. 69
Chandra, Bipin 6, 78
circular shrine 121, 124-25
Cunningham, Alexander 32

Das, Mahant Raghubar 65, 67, 69
Desai, ZA 114

Erskine, William 11

Fasanah-I Ibrat 50
Finch, William 17, 142
Fuhrer, Anton 3

Glazed tiles/ware 120, 128-29
Gobind Dev / Gobind Rai (temple) 8, 39-40
Godbole, Madhav 7
Gopal, S. 6, 78, 96
Goswami, Jiva 92-93
Govindachandra 104, 107-09, 126
Gumghasta Halat-i-Ajodhaya Awadh 52

Habib, Irfan 6-7, 52, 107, 110, 111, 115, 122, 127, 129, 143
Hadiqah-i Shuhada 49
Hafizullah 53
Hamilton, Walter 29
Hanuman Garhi 9, 10, 33, 49, 53-58
Hanuman Tila 1-2, 43-44
Hemadri Pandit 85
Herbert, Thomas 19
Husain, Kalab 72
Husian, Shah Ghulam 54

Ibrahim, Muhammad, Inspector of Waqf 73
interpolations/additions in the *khasra kishtwar* folios in the original Settlement Report of AD 1861 137

Jha, D.N. 6, 92, 98-99, 143
Jaisinghpuras 44
Jaiswal, Suvira 81-82
Jannah al-Mashriq wa Matla 'an-Nur al-Mashriq 2, 48
jizya 41
Joshi, M.C. 7, 97
Judgement on the Ramjanmabhumi/Babri Masjid Case 140

Kalidasa 82, 84-85
Kampana 36
Kapad-Dwar collection 44
Kautilya 85
Keshavdev temple 38
Khan, Justice S.U. 60, 63, 67, 135, 141
Krittivasa 34, 87
Kumaralata 85
Kunal, Kishore 6-7, 51, 93, 95, 98, 111-12

Laet, Joannes de 19
Lakshmidhara 108
Lal, B.B. 94-95, 97-102, 120
Leyden, John 11
Lime, mortar, surkhi 125

Madanmohan (Temple) 39
Maduravijaya 36
Mahavibhasha 85
Mandal, D. 101-02, 105, 122-23, 128-29, 131, 143
Marathas 40, 42
Martin, Robert Montgomery 29
Mathura 8, 11, 34, 37, 42, 44, 47, 49, 51, 126, 128-29
Maulana Abu l-Hasan 'Ali Nadawi 2, 48
maulud 1
Menon, Jaya 122, 125, 131-34, 143
Mettell, A.F. 58
mosque at Sambhal 13
mosque in Panipat 13
Muhammad, K.K. 5-6
Mukhlis, Anand Ram 15
Muraqqah-i Khusrawi 50

Nayar, K.K.K. 75
Nevill, H.R. 32, 58
Nirmohi Akhara 43, 64, 140, 141

Outram, James 53, 55

Pampa Ramayana 87
Pandit Hari Kishan 68
Pillar Bases 94, 96, 100-01, 118-19, 121-23, 126, 130-32
pranala 118, 121, 124

qanati mosque 126-28
Qaysar-u't Tawarikh 50

Ram Chabutara 60, 66, 129-30, 141
Ram, Chhabile 43
Rama Navami 23, 59, 64, 86
Ramacharitamanas 80, 83, 86, 87, 89, 105
Ramananda 86
Ramanandis (sect) 43, 52
Ramapurvatapaniya Upanishad 89
Ramarakshastotra of Budhakaushika 89
Ramesh, K.V. 103-04, 106-07
Ramjanmabhumi-Babri Masjid: A Historians'Report to the Nation 6-7
Ranganatha Ramayanam 87
Ratnagar, Shereen 102, 122-23
Ray, Newal 44
revenue records 136-37, 144
Riots in Ayodhya - 1912 70
Riots of 1934 71, 114
Roy, Sita Ram 122

Shah, Muhammad 15, 42, 44, 54
Shah, Wajid Ali 49, 51, 53-55, 57, 76
Sharma, R.S. 6, 79, 82, 92, 99, 126
Shrinathji 39
Shuaib, Maulvi 3-4, 113
Singh, Baghel 77
Singh, Sawai Jai 40-41, 43-45

Sita ki Rasoi 49-51, 53, 65-66, 70, 137-38, 140-41
Sridhara 90

Tarikh-i-Awadh (Hissa Doyam) 50, 52
tax on pilgrims 42
Thakran, R.C. 122-24
Thapar, Romila 6, 78-79, 96, 143
The Political Abuse of History: Babri Masjid-Ramjanmabhumi Dispute – An Analysis by Twenty-five Historians 78
Thornton, Edward 29
Tieffenthaler, Joseph 3, 20, 130, 142
Tirthakalpa 90
Treta Ka Thakur 7, 109-12
inscription 7, 111-12
Tulsidas 78, 80, 82, 86-87, 105

UP District Gazetteers – Faizabad (1960) 32

Verma, Supriya 122, 131-32, 143
Vishnu-Hari inscription 7
Vishwa Hindu Parishad (VHP) 5

Waqf 72-73, 114, 122, 138-39, 142, 144

Young, W. 70